PROMOTING HEALTH IN SCHOOLS

700030989985

PROMOTING HEALTH IN SCHOOLS

Emma Croghan

Paul Chapman Publishing

Paul Chapman Publishing
A SAGE Publications Company
1 Oliver's Yard
55 City Road
London EC1Y 1SP

SAGE Publications Inc
2455 Teller Road
Thousand Oaks, California 91320

SAGE Publications India Pvt Ltd
B 1/I 1 Mohan Cooperative Industrial Area
Mathura Road
New Delhi 110 044

SAGE Publications Asia-Pacific Pte Ltd
33 Pekin Street #02-01
Far East Square
Singapore 048763

Library of Congress Control Number: 2007922694

A catalogue record for this book is available from the British Library

ISBN-978-1-4129-2137-4
ISBN 978-1-4129-2138-1 (pbk)

Typeset by Pantek Arts Ltd, Maidstone, Kent
Printed in Great Britain by Cromwell Press Ltd, Trowbridge, Wiltshire
Printed on paper from sustainable resources

CONTENTS

ACKNOWLEDGEMENTS

This book is dedicated to my own children, Thomas, Charlotte and Katie, to my husband, Stuart, and to my parents, Colin and Elizabeth. I thank them for their continued support, encouragement and love.

This book is also dedicated to all of the hard-working colleagues in health, education and social care I have ever worked with.

PREFACE

This book comes at a time of immense change in education and health services. It is increasingly possible for both health and education staff to influence health and well-being outcomes for children and their families through partnership working and delivering creative services which support locally defined need. It is no longer the case that a 'one size fits all approach' prevails – rather there is an acceptance that what works in one area may not work in another, or indeed what works with one cohort of children or young people may not work with another. The National Healthy Schools Programme in England and Wales, and Health Promoting Schools in Scotland and Northern Ireland, offer opportunities and a framework for schools to assess, plan, implement and evaluate health promotion strategies in line with current policy context.

This book aims to support you as practitioners in education and health working with children aged from 3–11 in assessing the current situation, in assessing the available opportunities and risks in changing practice and in finding practical strategies to support personal, social and health education (PSHE) and wider school and community health promotion.

This book contains some background information and theory concerning aspects of health and health promotion to allow education and health staff to make informed and contemporarily relevant assessments of the current state of the school in relation to both Healthy Schools/ Health Promoting Schools status and in terms of the health enhancing environment.

The first part of this book (Chapters 1–5) aims to give information concerning whole-school approaches and provide background information for the reader. There are a number of exercises and activities for you to consider to self-assess and provide support for planning, implementing and evaluating activities.

The remaining chapters examine specific groups of primary school pupils (Early Years, Key Stage 1 and Key Stage 2, and their general physical, emotional and social health promotion needs, and aims to provide some ideas for activities and lessons to support them in learning how to become healthy children and, in future, healthy adults. Some of the lesson plans are suitable for use with all age groups, with more or less support from staff delivering the activity as necessary.

Throughout the book there are photocopiable resources for use in implementing health promotion activities.

The aim of the book is to provide the reader with an insight into:

- themes of physical, emotional and social health;

- a brief overview of the national schemes to promote health in schools across the UK;

- knowledge and resources to allow a whole-school assessment and plan a health promotion strategy across the whole primary school;

as well as providing:

- some example resources which can be used to carry out a programme to be run within the school framework to implement national standards in line with PSHE and citizenship curricula;

- some case studies as examples of good practice.

Aims of the book

The overall purpose of the book is to support the school and associated agencies to work together to develop and plan a whole-school approach to health promotion. The book offers a process of assessing, planning, implementing and evaluating practice, which starts with the development of a steering group.

It is advisable for schools to identify their local champions, such as the local Healthy Schools or Health Promoting Schools Coordinator, the school nurse and the local authority, to help and support their vision – there may be existing local funding or resources available for auditing, planning or evaluating such services. To identify your local champions, contact your local primary health care organisation, your local education authority and your local council, as well as possibly your local religious and voluntary organisations.

Lesson planning

All teachers know that planning is an essential element and skill involved in delivering effective teaching which results in effective learning. The content of each lesson and the learners of each lessons will often change, but general principles which lead to effective outcomes remain the same. However, for the benefit of non-teaching staff and others, the overarching principles of an effective plan outlined below will offer opportunity for:

- engagement with the students and the subject – an interesting introduction which is suitable for the developmental stage and age of the learner, and which piques continued interest;

- focused study – the clear focus of the lesson: this may be a new topic or area, or in fact may be revision of a previously taught area;

- contextualisation of the topic area within what is already known – where does this fit?

- tasks and activities which allow the student to reflect upon and apply the new learning in order to consolidate its context and position.

A lesson plan is a framework or guide to the objectives and outcomes hoped to be achieved in the lesson – what planning is to be done, why and how?

Although experienced teachers will have less need to formalise a full written plan, with a new subject area or less experience, more effort in planning can impact strongly on the teacher's confidence and focus for the lesson. Whether formalised as a written plan or thought through as an informal annotated process, thinking and following a clear process has a number of benefits:

- It allows for possible problems to be anticipated and solutions or options can then be considered.

- It increases confidence for the teacher.

- It ensures the lesson is balanced and has a clear rationale.

- It allows for a process of reflection following the lesson.

- It ensures the lesson is appropriate for the student group.

Even when there is a defined course content or course book, it is worth going through the planning process to provide an opportunity to think of alternatives or adaptations which may need to be made for some student groups.

The planning process

The following process demonstrates the key elements in the planning process:

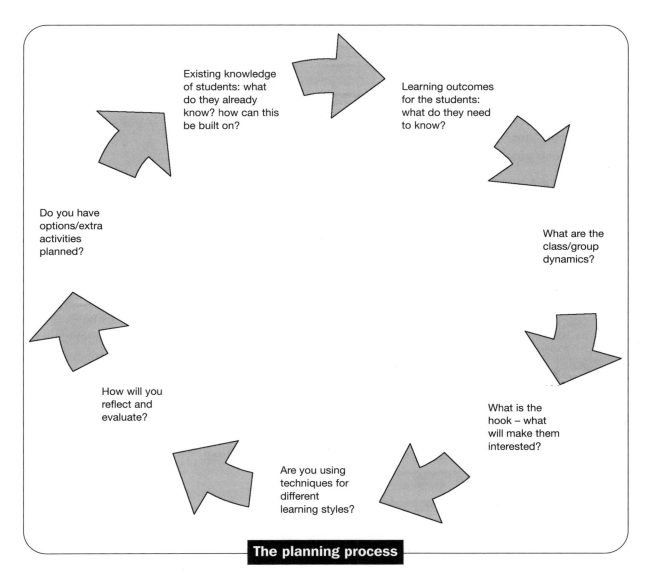

Existing knowledge of students: what do they already know? how can this be built on?

Learning outcomes for the students: what do they need to know?

What are the class/group dynamics?

What is the hook – what will make them interested?

Are you using techniques for different learning styles?

How will you reflect and evaluate?

Do you have options/extra activities planned?

The planning process

1   What are you trying to achieve? Do you have clear and concise aims? Are they realistic? Consider the following questions:
    (a)   What do the students know already?
    (b)   What do the students need to know?
    (c)   What did you do with the students in the previous class?
    (d)   Do you know the class dynamics?
    (e)   Do you know how motivated the students are?

2 Does your lesson plan have enough variety? Is there more than one technique of delivery – do the children have the opportunity to listen, talk, move about or touch something?

3 Have you built in any flexibility? If an activity does not last as long as you thought, or if it is not appropriate at the time of the lesson, are there extra or alternative activities you could do which reinforce the learning outcomes?

4 What is the hook to pique their interest/engage them?

5 Have you built in the opportunity to contextualise the new information with what is already known?

6 How will you evaluate each element and activity – how will you test the learning outcomes and your aims?

7 How will it be followed up and supported in the longer term?

Strategies for delivering health promotion

The learning environment

The environment in which the child or pupil is exposed to new information or education provides triggers and reinforcement to the content of the teaching. It consists of the physical environment, how it is arranged and furnished, the materials and equipment which are available, any planned and unplanned activities, and the people who are present, as well as any regular routines. The learning environment can be improved by keeping messages simple, by not having too many distractions or new elements and, when new elements are introduced, by keeping some of the existing and consistent elements.

Warm-up activities

It is often useful to start a lesson with a warm-up activity – integrating this with the need to engage the pupils and pique interest, as described earlier. Some examples of this are starter questions with group feedback, brainstorming by asking children to shout out ideas and recording them on a board, or by asking children to brainstorm ideas against a particular theme, such as 'any words you can think of about food which begin with the letter A', or for younger children 'any foods you can think of which are red'.

Drama, and role play

Drama can be an integral method for helping children to empathise, understand a different perspective, become independent or try out an idea within a safe context. For drama and role play techniques to be integrated they need to be linked into the context of the lesson with an understanding of and connection to the following:

- the identity/roles of the people involved in the situation;

- the time and place of the events;

- a focus or issue that concerned the people involved.

Potential dramatic interpretative strategies could include;

- focusing on a still image;

- overheard conversations;

- forums and debate;

- meetings;

- moving into another person's seat and seeing things from their perspective;

- reinterpretation of a story identifying with a particular character.

Questions

Questions can either be open or closed in style. A closed question is one in which the answer is driven and is usually dichotomous, e.g. for the question 'is your name Thomas?' the answer can only be 'yes', 'no', or possibly 'I don't know'. As such, closed questions can be useful for checking understanding and testing recall. Open questions are often more useful as they elicit views and promote discussion, they explore perception and increase curiosity.

Trigger questions are similar to open questions, but with more focus allowing for specific development of a planned theme, e.g. 'what could go wrong with this?', 'what could they do differently?'

Key questions drive the focus of the topic and act as overarching topic questions, e.g. 'what do we need to be healthy?' Key questions should only be the important thematic questions which can bring coherence to the structure of the lesson.

Offering pupils the opportunity to ask questions allows them the opportunity to test their individual learning and to check their understanding of context and content.

All of these questioning techniques can be usefully employed in individual lessons.

The lesson plans and teaching and learning styles

Each lesson plan provided in this book develops a health promotion theme through short-term activities within one longer lesson period. It is advisable to split the lessons into smaller activities, particularly with younger children, to provide regular breaks and reinforcement, as well as to defuse any tensions. Each set of activities within each lesson plan offers activities which fulfil one of the VAK learning styles – providing opportunities for visual, auditory and kinaesthetic (movement) stimuli within the wider theme of the lesson. Lesson plans may need to be adapted to suit the local cultural needs of the children and families. Where outside partners such as parents carers and others are invited in to participate in the lesson, it is suggested that they are each assigned to a small group to help with the targeted nature of the activities – to refocus and ask prompting questions to the children in 'their' groups.

Follow-up to pupil questions

Offering follow-up opportunities to put questions without embarrassing or identifying pupils can be problematic. The use of techniques such as question boxes can be used prior to or following specific lessons and can allow the questions of individuals to be answered without personal identification. A question box, as the name suggests, describes a box which can be used to put questions in which the teacher can seal so that questions cannot be withdrawn.

LIST OF ABBREVIATIONS

CAMHS	Child and Adolescent Mental Health Services
CPD	continuing professional development
CWDC	Children's Workforce Development Council
DfEE	Department for Education and Employment
DfES	Department for Education and Skills
DoH	Department of Health
ECM	Every Child Matters
HPS	Health Promoting School
HSA	home–school agreement
HSC	Health and Safety Commission
HSE	Health and Safety Executive
ICT	information and communications technology
INSET	in-service training
LEA	local education authority
NHSP	National Healthy Schools Programme
NNEB	National Nursery Examination Board
NSF	National Service Framework
Ofsted	Office for Standards in Education
ONS	Office of National Statistics
PASS	Pupil Attitude to School and Health
PSHE	personal, social and health education
RoSPA	Royal Society for the Prevention of Accidents
SAT	standard assessment test
SEAL	Social and Emotional Aspects of Learning
SEF	self-evaluation framework

SEN	special educational needs
SENCO	Special Educational Needs Coordinator
SEU	Social Exclusion Unit
SRE	sex and relationship education
VAK	visual, auditory and kinaesthetic
WHO	World Health Organisation

CHECKLIST OF PHOTOCOPIABLE PAGES

Chapter 6

Chapter 7

Chapter 8

Chapter 9

CHAPTER 1

The whole-school approach to health promotion

> **Chapter aims**
>
> This chapter shows you how to identify your school's current strengths and weaknesses in relation to promoting health in the school environment. It also helps you to understand the context and content of health promotion in its widest sense and the national schemes which might be suitable for you to work within.

Health promotion in schools is a contemporary and important issue, frequently highlighted through media campaigns, whether focusing on school meals, sexual health promotion or bullying and emotional health. There is a great deal of information about why health promotion in schools is important and there is also a lot of very good practice going on: the aim of this book is to provide a practical resource of tried and tested methods and mechanisms for the delivery of health promoting activities in primary school contexts.

Any health promotion activity cannot occur in isolation: all messages need to be reinforced throughout both school and home interactions. This requires the engagement and involvement of all school staff, from lunchtime supervisors to administrative staff, as well as parents and carers. Again, this book aims to provide practical mechanisms for supporting and delivering this.

Policy context

Contemporary policy context

The Department of Health (DoH) document *Choosing Health* (2004a) states the aim that each secondary school and its feeder cluster of primary schools should have a named school nurse. This will be a qualified general nurse, often with other qualifications, who is able to support the health needs of children as well as the strategic development of health promotion in schools, through examples such as the delivery of health education, support for policy writing, community work and the identification of health issues. The latest policy guidance from the Department of

Education and Skills, the Department of Culture, Media and Sport, the Treasury and the Department of Health in England and Wales suggests partnership working between health, education and other relevant partners to achieve healthy school status and outcomes. Providing easier access to all types of services in areas where children and young people spend most of their time is key to the Every Child Matters (ECM) five key objectives of ensuring that children:

- stay safe;

- are healthy;

- enjoy and achieve;

- make a positive contribution; and

- achieve economic well-being (ECM – see website).

These five key objectives underpin a shared philosophy in England and Wales, published under Every Child Matters, which ensures that promoting the health and well-being of children, young people and their families is at the heart of all provision, whichever agency is the main deliverer of services.

Supporting health, education and social care outcomes in line with the five core objectives of Every Child Matters led to the further development of the Extended Schools programme. This programme had its roots in a full-service schools approach developed and implemented initially in the US and first implemented in the UK in Scotland in 1999. English policy development was initiated through a document published by the Social Exclusion Unit in 1998, which was followed by Pathfinder work and was formalised as part of the ECM strategy. In 2005, the Extended Schools prospectus provided a core offer of services, centred around and based within a school, that all children and young people should be able to access fully by 2010. The current core offer is shown below.

- high quality 'wraparound' childcare provided on the school site or through other local providers, with supervised transfer arrangements where appropriate, available 8am–6pm all year round

- a varied menu of activities to be on offer such as homework clubs and study support, sport (at least two hours a week beyond the school day for those who want it), music tuition, dance and drama, arts and crafts, special interest clubs such as chess and first aid courses, visits to museums and galleries, learning a foreign language, volunteering, business and enterprise activities

- parenting support including information sessions for parents at key transition points, parenting programmes run with the support of other children's services and family learning sessions to allow children to learn with their parents

- swift and easy referral to a wide range of specialist support services such as speech therapy, child and adolescent mental health services, family support services, intensive behavioural support, and (for older young people) sexual health services. Some may be delivered on school sites

- providing wider community access to ICT, sports and arts facilities, including adult learning

Schools will want to work closely with parents to shape these activities around the needs of their community and may choose to provide extra services in response to parental demand. The core offer ensures that all children and parents have access to a minimum of services and activities. 'Extended School' is not a status that schools centrally apply for as there is no blueprint for the types of activities that schools might offer.

Some of these services such as health and social care will be provided free of charge. These sorts of services will need to be funded often by local authorities and their children's trust partners such as Primary Care Trusts. But for other services, such as childcare, charges will need to be made. Schools or the partners that they are working with will need to devise charging regimes that cover the costs of the services but that are affordable for working parents. (DfES, 2005a: 8)

Children's Workforce and the Common Core

Every Child Matters (see website) and the development of policy and programmes to support it has led to the further development of coordinated packages of care, such as the Extended Schools programme outlined above. The rational conclusion to this work is the development of a shared multidisciplinary workforce – the children's workforce, with common core skills and knowledge. Further information about the development of the children's workforce can be obtained from the Children's Workforce Development Council (CWDC) at http://www.cwdcouncil.org.uk/aboutcwdc/index.htm.

The Common Core of Skills and Knowledge (DFES/DoH, 2005a) ensures that all professionals working with children share common areas of knowledge. The Common Core for the Children's Workforce contains standards in the following key areas:

- effective communication;
- child and young person development;
- safeguarding and promoting child welfare;
- supporting transitions;
- multi agency working;
- sharing information.

More information about the Common Core can be found at the Every Child Matters website: http://www.everychildmatters.gov.uk/deliveringservices/commoncore/.

Health and schools: a potted history

The 1899–90 recruitment drive for male volunteers to serve in the Boer War highlighted a worrying lack of physically able young men in the UK, with nearly 35 per cent of all volunteer recruits being declared physically unfit for duty. At the same time, the work of social reformers such as Joseph Rowntree was leading to a widespread conviction that health and social class were inversely related. Rowntree demonstrated that the lowest classes received on average about 25 per cent less food than considered nutritionally adequate and that one-fifth of the children in Glasgow were found to have rickets due to malnutrition. This awareness led to the formation of the Interdepartmental Committee on Physical Deterioration in 1904. The purpose of the committee was firstly to establish, with the help of the medical profession, methods to measure the health of the population; secondly to suggest the causes of the physical deterioration of the nation; and thirdly to suggest the most provident methods for improving the nation's health.

Two main paradigms for health improvement among school populations prevailed throughout the early 1900s: firstly, the work and beliefs of eugenics experts; and secondly, the public health work of epidemiologists and environmental health workers. These two paradigms divided the committee for some time into a group who believed that the children of the UK had deteriorated through poor genetic inheritance, and those who believed that poor sanitary, environmental and public health issues along with poverty were the root causes of the physical ill health of the nation.

Eventually persuaded by the public health argument, the committee made more than fifty recommendations to improve the health of the public, many of which were aimed at improving the health of school-aged youth and young parents. This is, in reality, the beginning of an ongoing battle to improve health and well-being outcomes for children and young people, which is currently centred in the UK around National Healthy Schools Schemes.

Timeline of health and schools convergence

1899	Boer War recruitment drive highlights poor public health issues of school leavers
1907	Education (Administrative Provision) Act provides a framework for public health surveillance in schools
1908	Children Act gives protection and rights to children who previously had none, legislates against parental neglect and abuse and provides free school meals
1944	Amended Education Act ensures all children have access to health screening at school
1945	Handicapped Pupils and School Health Regulations requires all school nurses to hold the Health Visitor qualification and to be known as School Health Visitors
1973	Managerial control of school health services passes from local education authorities (LEAs) to health authorities UN Rights of the Child The Children Act
1989	Healthy Schools Schemes first seen in Europe
1997	School nurses identified as leading 'child-centred public health'
1998	National Healthy Schools Programme (NHSP) funded
2003	*Every Child Matters* Green Paper
2004	*Every Child Matters* White Paper
2005	*Youth Matters* published (DfES, 2005b) National Service Framework for Children Young People and Maternity Services Common Core of Knowledge and Skills
2006	Children's Workforce development consultation

Schools and national health promotion schemes

Healthy Schools Schemes were first seen in Europe in 1989, when a 'health promoting school' was considered one in which:

- time is allocated to health-related issues in the formal curriculum through subjects including home economics, physical education, social education and health studies;

- health remains the hidden curriculum of the school including staff/pupil relationships, school/community relationships, the school environment and the quality of services such as school meals;

- the health and caring services visit the school, providing a health promotion role in the school through screening, prevention and child guidance.

These principles remain fundamental to achieving a health-promoting school and achieving the National Healthy Schools Award for your school. If you would like to achieve this award, these are questions you should ask of yourself, your activities and your wider school to support your application.

In the UK, two national programmes, Health Promoting Schools (in Scotland) and the National Healthy Schools Programme (NHSP in England and Wales), were launched to allow schools a structured framework to develop their health promotion agenda.

> 'A health promoting school is one in which all members of the school community work together to provide children and young people with integrated and positive experiences and structures, which promote and protect their health. This includes both the formal and the informal curriculum in health, the creation of a safe and healthy school environment, the provision of appropriate health services and the involvement of the family and wider community in efforts to promote health.' (WHO, 1995)

The National Healthy School Standard, now the National Healthy Schools Programme (NHSP), was originally (in the late 1990s) jointly funded by the Department for Education and Skills (DfES) and the Department of Health (DoH), and it remains a collaborative programme. The overall aim of both NHSP and the Scottish Health Promoting Schools programme is to help schools become effective at providing an environment that is conducive to being healthy and learning, and that ultimately encourages pupils to achieve to their individual potential.

National Healthy Schools Programme

The NHSP is an accreditation from the Department for Education and Skills (formerly the Department for Education and Employment) which had at inception three core aims:

1 Reducing inequalities in health

2 Promoting social inclusion

3 Raising educational attainment. (NHSP 2005)

These were updated and refined in 2005 to the following:

1 To support children and young people in developing healthy lifestyle behaviours

2 To support and raise pupil achievement

3 To help promote social inclusion and social health

4 To assist in reducing health and social inequalities. (DfES/DoH, 2005b)

It has at its centre ten *areas* of whole-school improvements and four core *themes*. Schools can choose which of the themes they plan to address initially (following an audit, preferably, to show which areas are the priority); they then need to ensure the theme is implemented in each area (see Figure 1.1).

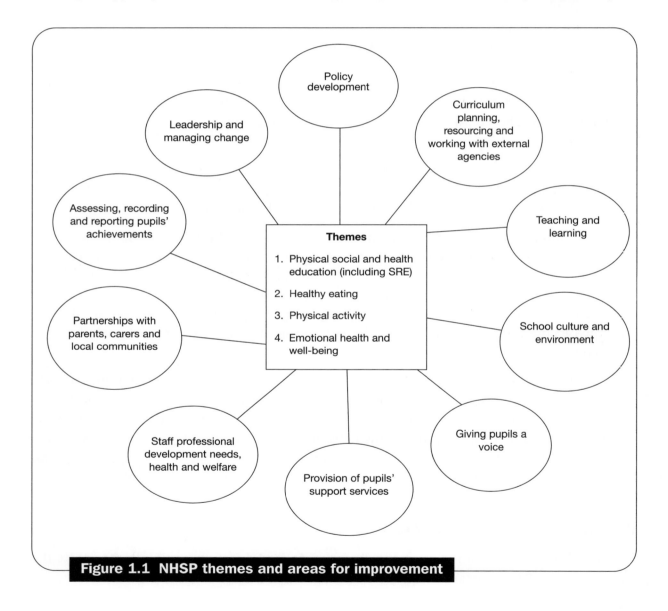

Figure 1.1 NHSP themes and areas for improvement

By 2009 all schools will be working towards healthy schools status, as healthy schools are seen as a key driver for delivering some of the public health outcomes identified for children and young people. It is being extended from primary and secondary schools to all educational establishments, including nursery and early years provision, colleges and further education and is fundamental within the Extended Schools programme. Both teachers and nurses can undertake a certification programme through NHSP in teaching PSHE. Further information about the certification programme and the NHSP can be found at the Wired for Health website, the website of the NHSP, coordinated by both the DfES and the DoH: http://www.wiredforhealth.gov.uk.

Ofsted and health

The Office for Standards in Education (Ofsted) acts as an independent inspection mechanism for all state-funded educational establishments. The inspection framework was updated in 2005 in light of the publication of *Every Child Matters* (see website). Under section 5 of the Education Act 2005 the mandatory areas to be reported upon by inspectors are:

- the quality of the education provided in the school;

- how far the education meets the needs of the range of pupils at the school;

- the educational standards achieved in the school;

- the quality of the leadership and management of the school, including whether the financial resources made available to the school are managed efficiently;

- the spiritual, moral, social and cultural development of the pupils at the school;

- the contribution made by the school to the well-being of those pupils (Ofsted, 2005).

Clearly the health and well-being of the school pupils is an integral part of the inspection process.

PSHE and its relevance to health promotion

The personal, social and health education curriculum allows all schools to take a holistic approach to health and well-being, whether aiming for a Healthy School award or not. It provides a loose framework for a needs-led locally defined curriculum which supports children in defining their own values concerning holistic health and well-being. Personal education relates mainly to emotional literacy and well-being, health education relates to providing knowledge and skills around physical health and social health relates to community and group cohesion and understanding.

The National Healthy Schools programme standards relating to PSHE are as follows:

- The school recognises that all aspects of school life have an impact on the personal and social development of pupils and that consistent messages are presented.

- The school encourages pupils to recognise their achievement and do their best (DoH, 2005a).

Health promoting schools also include PSHE provision as an indicator of achievement:

- development in pupils of positive attitudes and personal and social skills;
- contribution of extra-curricular activities, syllabus inserts and special courses.

A non-statutory framework for PSHE has been developed through the National Curriculum (see website) which contains four key areas for increasing knowledge, skills and understanding within PSHE at Key Stage 1:

- Developing confidence and responsibility and making the most of their abilities
- Preparing to play an active role as citizens
- Developing a healthy, safer lifestyle
- Developing good relationships and respecting the differences between people.

What is health promotion?

Health promotion centres on the initial premise that health is not 'merely the absence of disease or infirmity', but 'a state of complete physical, mental and social well-being'.[1] This statement has often been criticised for being oversimplistic and difficult to attain as it relies on complete well-being. For example, a child who had an accident and is a wheelchair user may not ever again be considered, under this definition, to be healthy. This led to further developments in the theory and practice of health promotion and health improvement.

Within the contexts of enabling and empowering human beings to make positive choices, two main theoretical and practical movements were formed, broadly divided into health education and health promotion. Health education is now considered to be a key element within the wider boundaries of effective health promotion activity.

Health promotion has since been defined by the World Health Organisation (WHO) as a broad doctrine which encompasses healthy public policy, creating supportive environments, strengthening community action, and supporting and developing personal skills. The WHO's Ottawa Charter for Health Promotion (1986) clarified the nature of health promotion, defining it as 'the process of enabling people to increase control over, and to improve, their health'.

Overall it seems that health promotion can be defined as helping people develop or change lifestyle habits which support long-term optimal health outcomes, whether they are related to emotional, physical, intellectual or spiritual well-being. There are three dimensions to this:

- raising awareness and providing information (health education);
- behavioural change support;
- providing supportive environments to enhance positive choices and practices.

---

1   Preamble to the Constitution of the World Health Organisation as adopted by the International Health Conference, New York, 19–22 June 1946; signed on 22 July 1946 by the representatives of 61 States (Official Records of the World Health Organisation, no. 2, p. 100) and entered into force on 7 April 1948.

In terms of primary schools this means that we write and police policies which are broadly:

- health enhancing (i.e. allowing children to drink from personal water bottles throughout the day, having a non-smoking school site);

- providing and supporting environments which are supportive of positive health choices (offering parents information about local stop smoking services, not having squash provided at lunchtime, providing information about the benefits of drinking water for parents and carers, teaching children about those benefits);

- strengthening community action through community activities (providing a community location for a stop smoking group, lobbying leisure centres to provide water fountains and get rid of carbonated drinks machines, etc.); and

- supporting the development of personal skill acquisition in both children and their parents or family by providing information and reinforcing messages at every opportunity.

Why be involved in school-based health promotion activity?

Whether through a national scheme or otherwise, there is clear evidence that holistic school-based approaches to delivering health promotion in schools has a positive impact on pupils, the wider school, staff and wider communities. National schemes have been shown, through their structure and processes, to improve outcomes in both health and education. Schools which are part of the NHSP have been shown to be improving both health and education outcomes of pupils at a faster rate than non-NHSP schools (DfES, 2004b). As well as this, the DfES publication *Healthy Living Blueprint for Schools* (2004a) carries five aims for progress. The aim is for all schools to make progress with:

1 promoting a school ethos and environment which encourage a healthy lifestyle

2 using the full capacity and flexibility of the curriculum to achieve a healthy lifestyle

3 ensuring that the food and drink available across the school day reinforce the healthy lifestyle message

4 providing high quality physical education and school sport and promoting physical activity as part of a lifelong healthy lifestyle

5 promoting an understanding of the full range of issues and behaviours which impact upon lifelong health.

School policies and health

School policies can be usefully employed to help support health promotion in schools and early years environments. Key policies relating to health promotion are:

- medicines management;

- behaviour and attendance;

- bullying.

Using guidance such as the DfES's *Healthy Living Blueprint for Schools* (2004a) ensures that these policies are embedded within, and add to, the health promoting ethos of the school. Some medicines and long-term medical conditions management support is available from http://publications.teachernet.gov.uk/default.aspx?PageFunction=productdetails&PageMode= publications&ProductId=DFES-1448-2005.

The importance of a preliminary assessment – how and why

As has previously been described, one of the key elements of health promotion in schools is ensuring the school environment itself provides opportunity for health enhancement. As well as this, to be able to offer a 'health promoting school' to pupils, an understanding and assessment of the needs of the wider school community is needed. Below, forms are provided which can be completed to allow an understanding of the health needs of the school. This will allow for planning health promotion activity. An idea of where to gather the required information is also provided. The most appropriate way to complete the first of these might be to work in a group, including the headteacher (or other member of school senior management team), school cook, school governor, PSHE lead and school nurse. This can be used with the planning questions to identify priorities for the school health promotion plan.

The school health promotion plan

To support your wider school community as well as any work to improve health outcomes for pupils and their families, you will need to create a health promotion plan. This plan will need to cover the rationale for delivering activities against an evaluation plan. It will also need to consider each planned activity and a decision must be made whether it falls into the context of:

- raising awareness and providing information (health education);

- behavioural change and support;

Or:

- providing supportive environments to enhance positive choices and practice?

Evaluation of your current status and your interventions

The plan needs to include how you will evaluate the health promotion in your school to decide whether it was effective or not. Evaluating health promotion is complex, as often the outcomes are not seen for many years, and other things may have happened outside of your intervention which might have affected the outcome. The Scottish governmental document, *How Good is Our School?* (http://www.scotland.gov.uk/library2/doc08/rthp-02.htm) provides an overview for evaluating school health promotion, based on self-evaluation by school staff. As a minimum, any evaluation of a health promotion intervention should include a consideration of:

- the process – how effective was the way in which the activity was delivered? could it have been done differently?

- the outcomes – changes to awareness, knowledge, attitudes or behaviour;

- the relevance – if voluntary, did people come/attend?

- cost-effectiveness – how much did it cost to deliver the activity? did it prevent something else being done which might have had more effect?

This can then be used to inform future planning as well as provide evidence to support or withdraw continued involvement with the activity you delivered.

Tying it up with self-evaluation frameworks

Although the evaluation provided here is a simplistic and health-led assessment, it could be used by education staff within the self-evaluation framework (SEF). The main areas where the SEF and the health assessment can be used together and to inform each other are:

- Section 1 (d) and (e) – student and school characteristics and school priorities.

- Section 2 (d) – actions taken due to stakeholder views and input.

- Section 4 personal development and well-being.

Where to start

It is best to start with the two school assessment plans overleaf, and use these as a baseline from which to move on. This provides an overview of both the environmental and physical health challenges and catalysts which are currently seen in your school. There is an outline plan for schools to complete to give a clear picture of what, why and when interventions will be delivered.

Assessing the School Health Needs 1: The School Community

To be completed by the assessment team

Item	Numbers (%)	Where to get information
Number of male pupils on the register		School records
Number of female pupils on the register		School records
Number of white pupils on the register		School records
Number of Afro-Caribbean pupils on the register		School records
Number of South Asian pupils on the register		School records
Number of other ethnic pupils on the register		School records
Number of pupils on the register with a physical impairment		School records
Number of pupils on the SEN register		SENCO
Number of pupils with English as a second language		School records
Number of pupils with two parents/carers at home		School records
Main reasons for attendance at A&E		Three-month tally of A&E slips: school nurse
Headteacher's perceptions of main health issues		Headteacher

PSHE coordinator's perceptions of main health issues		PSHE lead
School nurse's perceptions of main health issues		School nurse
Pupils' perceptions of main health issues		Ask 2/3 pupils from each year
Parental perceptions of main health issues		Ask parents
Number of obese/overweight pupils		School nurse
Numbers of pupils eligible for free school meals		School records
Numbers of pupils taking school meals		School records
Parental involvement methods		Headteacher

Assessing the School Health Needs 1: The School Community (Example)

Example completed by the assessment team

Item	Numbers (%)	Where to get information
Number of male pupils on the register	49%	School records
Number of female pupils on the register	51%	School records
Number of white pupils on the register	96%	School records
Number of Afro-Caribbean pupils on the register	1%	School records
Number of South Asian pupils on the register	2%	School records
Number of other ethnic pupils on the register	1%	School records
Number of pupils on the register with a physical impairment	2 (1%)	School records
Number of pupils on the SEN register	20 (10%)	SENCO
Number of pupils with English as an additional language	4 (2%)	School records
Number of pupils with two parents/carers at home	180 (90%)	School records
Main reasons for attendance at A&E	1. Accidents (falls/slips/cuts) 2. Accidental burns 3. Nausea and vomiting	Three-month tally of A&E slips: school nurse
Headteacher's perceptions of main health issues	Accident prevention Children attending school with infectious coughs/colds/stomach bugs Healthy eating	Headteacher

Paul Chapman Publishing 2007 © Emma Croghan

Assessing the School Health Needs 1: The School Community (Example)

PSHE coordinator's perceptions of main health issues	Emotional health and bullying Healthy eating Spread of infectious coughs/colds/stomach bugs	PSHE lead
School nurse's perceptions of main health issues	Accident prevention Emotional health and bullying Sickness absence	School nurse
Pupils' perceptions of main health issues	Drinking water not available to all More opportunity to be active Better lunch options	Ask 2/3 pupils from each year
Parental perceptions of main health issues	Healthy eating Bullying	Ask parents
Number of obese/overweight pupils	Overweight: 40 (20%) Obese 9 (5%)	School nurse
Number of pupils eligible for free school meals	20 (10%)	School records
Number of pupils taking school meals	160 (80%)	School records
Parental involvement methods	Home–school diaries (daily) Termly meetings Opportunistic meeting with teachers	Headteacher

Assessing the School Health Needs 2: The School Environment

To be completed by the assessment team

Item	Numbers (%), information or yes/no	Where to get information
Numbers of toilets		School walk round
Numbers of hand washing facilities		School walk round
Are there facilities for the physically impaired?		School walk round
Is there sanitary towel provision for pupils		School walk round
Description of locality around school (type of road, ease of access, etc.)		School walk round
Description of school grounds (any broken areas, health hazards, grassy areas, positive health areas)		
Healthy school award attained or aiming towards?		NHSP coordinator HT
Number of pupils and staff who walk to school		School count 2 mornings
Number of pupils and staff who cycle to school		School count 2 mornings

What exercise opportunities are there?		School
Is fast food provided?		School cook
Number of vending machines selling sugary drinks/ chocolates, etc.		School
Types of healthy snacks available		
Average number of fruit portions not consumed per week		Assess numbers left each day for one week
Average number of pupils eating fruit in packed lunch		Assess contents of lunchboxes over 2–5 days
Is water available in school at all times for pupils to drink?		School walk round

Assessing the School Health Needs 2: The School Environment (Example)

Example completed by the assessment team

Item	Numbers (%), information or yes/no	Where to get information
Numbers of toilets	1 block – 4 toilets for girls, 2 toilets and urinal for boys	School walk round
Numbers of hand washing facilities	4 sinks in each toilet with bar soap and paper towels. Each classroom has sink with liquid soap and paper towels.	School walk round
Are there facilities for the physically impaired?	Staff toilet is suitable. Work planned for this year to create new toilet block with facility for physically impaired.	School walk round
Is there sanitary towel provision for pupils?	On request from teacher. Disposal bin in staff toilet only.	School walk round
Description of locality around school (type of road, ease of access, etc.)	Based just off main road of village. Busy with cars at drop off and collection times. Crossing patrol people at 3 sites. Large green area to back of school.	School walk round
Description of school grounds (any broken areas, health hazards, grassy areas, positive health areas)	Large fields for playing on. Sheltered play areas x2. Sandpit available. Broken area by gate into school, gate also has a sticking out piece – to be mended asap.	
Healthy school award attained or aiming towards?	Aiming towards.	NHSP coordinator HT
Number of pupils and staff who walk to school	15% of pupils walk all the way to school 59% walk some or part of the way 2 teachers (20%) walk to school	School count 2 mornings

Assessing the School Health Needs 2: The School Environment (Example)

Number of pupils and staff who cycle to school	No staff 10 pupils (5%)	School count 2 mornings
What exercise opportunities are there?	Grassy area – free play at breaks and lunchtime. Organised activities at lunchtime – organised by supervisory staff. Skipping ropes and footballs provided. After school dancing, gym and football clubs – free of charge.	School
Is fast food provided?	Burgers once per week Chips once per week	School cook
Number of vending machines selling sugary drinks/ chocolates, etc.	None	School
Types of healthy snacks available	Salad available every day Fruit and yoghurt available every day Milk and water provided at lunchtime Daily fruit offered to all children	
Average number of fruit portions not consumed per week	20% left most days Most commonly left – tomato	Assess numbers left each day for one week
Average number of pupils eating fruit in packed lunch	90% of pupils had fruit in lunchbox.	Assess contents of lunchboxes over 2–5 days
Is water available in school at all times for pupils to drink?	Pupils may ask for a drink from the teacher, but rarely do.	School walk round

Assessing the School Health Promotion Summary

To be completed by the assessment team

1. What were the three main reasons identified why pupils at the school attended hospital?

2. What health promotion activities could you undertake to address each of these?

3. What are the main environmental issues which need addressing and how could you achieve this?

4. Did the health perceptions differ between the pupils, parents, teachers, nurse and headteacher? If so, how? How could this be addressed? Were there areas of commonality? If so, what?

School Health Promotion Plan

Aims:

Short-term objectives (what you will aim to achieve by next term):

- raising awareness and providing information (health education)?

- behavioural change or support?

- providing supportive environments to enhance positive choices and practice?

What themes (NHSP) does the activity cover and how can it contribute to whole-school improvement?

	Areas of whole-school improvement									
Theme	1	2	3	4	5	6	7	8	9	10

Why is this important?

Methods (how you will do it):

School Health Promotion Plan

To be completed by the assessment team

Short-term objectives (what you will aim to achieve in two terms):

- raising awareness and providing information (health education)?
- behavioural change or support?
- providing supportive environments to enhance positive choices and practice?

What themes (NHSP) does the activity cover and how can it contribute to whole-school improvement?

Theme	Areas of whole-school improvement									
	1	2	3	4	5	6	7	8	9	10

Why is this important?

Methods (how you will do it):

School Health Promotion Plan

To be completed by the assessment team

Long-term objectives (what you will aim to achieve in one year):

- raising awareness and providing information (health education)?

- behavioural change or support?

- providing supportive environments to enhance positive choices and practice?

What themes (NHSP) does the activity cover and how can it contribute to whole-school improvement?

	Areas of whole-school improvement									
Theme	1	2	3	4	5	6	7	8	9	10

Why is this important?

Methods (how you will do it):

To be completed by the assessment team

Evaluation plan (how you will decide if it worked):

The process – how effective was the way in which the activity was delivered? Could it have been done differently?

The outcomes – awareness, knowledge, attitudes or behaviour? How can you measure this?

The relevance – if voluntary, did people come/attend?

Cost-effectiveness – how much did it cost to deliver the activity? Did it prevent something else being done which might have had more effect?

Self-Evaluation of Current Status

Use this with the schools Self-Evaluation Framework (SEF) to identify your school's current strengths and weaknesses relating to the various areas of a health promoting school agenda.

Scoring

4 This is something we are very good at – one of our major strengths.

3 This is something we are OK at – our strengths outweigh our weaknesses.

2 This is something which needs further development, but which we have made a start with.

1 This is a major weakness which needs major work and development.

Themes	Self-assessed score
Health and well-being are integrated across the curriculum.	
There is clear support and guidance for teachers around aspects of health and well-being and they are clear what the learning and health outcomes and agendas are.	
There is a good and age-appropriate choice of tasks, activities and resources.	
There is a clear pace of learning to achieve appropriate targets for all pupils.	
All staff are involved as and where appropriate.	
There is clear provision for the emotional, physical and social needs of individual pupils.	
Extra curricular activities and outside agencies are integrated into the curriculum.	
The school has a sense of community and belonging.	
There is encouragement of parents to be involved in their child's learning and the life of the school.	
The school is responsive to parents' and carer's views and enquiries.	
School governors are involved in developing or delivering the wider health promoting agenda.	
Local, voluntary and other organisations visit the school and contribute to the health and well-being agenda.	
Resources and supplementary work is displayed and used to support the curriculum work around health and well-being.	

CHAPTER 2

Promotion of physical health and well-being in classrooms

Chapter aims

The aim of this chapter is to provide some ideas for professionals about how to promote physical health in the classroom. It includes ideas for activities to undertake, as well as the rationale for undertaking them, within the context of promoting physical health and well-being.

Healthy schools national schemes

The NHSP in England and Wales and Health Promoting Schools in Scotland and Northern Ireland identify the importance of the promotion of physical health and well-being in schools. A healthy school promotes 'the health and wellbeing of its pupils and staff through a well planned, taught curriculum in a physical and emotional environment that promotes learning and healthy lifestyle choices'. (Denman et al., 2002: 4).

Within the ten areas for whole-school improvement, the rights of workers are considered in the following:

- School culture and environment
- Staff professional development needs, health and welfare.

The rights of pupils are also considered in these areas:

- School culture and environment
- Teaching and learning.

Within the context of health promoting schools, physical health and safety is paramount, particularly in the following areas:

- Pastoral care
- Provision of accommodation and facilities
- Organisation and use of resources and space.

It is therefore important that schools and other associated agencies such as health care providers have an overview of the legal position relating to physical health and well-being.

Schools as employers: the law and health promotion

In the United Kingdom, the law is clear about the rights of workers to a health-enhancing and protective environment which does not prove detrimental to physical, social or psychological well-being. The Health and Safety at Work Act 1974 places overall responsibility for health and safety with the employer. It is enforced by the Health and Safety Executive (HSE).

In particular the law states that it is the employer's responsibility to:

- make the workplace safe and without risks to health;
- ensure plant and machinery are safe and that safe systems of work are set up and followed;
- ensure articles and substances are moved, stored and used safely;
- provide adequate welfare facilities;
- provide the information, instruction, training and supervision necessary for employee health and safety.

This must include an assessment of risk (written or recorded with planned arrangements for change where necessary when there are five or more employees), the appointment of someone deemed 'competent' to support the health and safety of employees, setting up emergency procedures, providing adequate first aid facilities and communicating all of this to staff in a way that is accessible to all.

The employer must also comply with health, safety and welfare requirements relating to the provision of ventilation, stable temperature, lighting, sanitation, washing and rest facilities.

The employer must also:

- ensure that work equipment is suitable for its intended use, so far as health and safety is concerned, and that it is properly maintained and used;
- prevent or adequately control exposure to substances which may damage health;
- take precautions against danger from flammable or explosive hazards, electrical equipment, noise and radiation;
- avoid hazardous manual handling operations, and where they cannot be avoided, reduce the risk of injury;
- provide free any protective clothing or equipment, where risks are not adequately controlled by other means;
- ensure that appropriate safety signs are provided and maintained;

- report certain injuries, diseases and dangerous occurrences to the appropriate health and safety enforcing authority.

Finally, the employer must provide health surveillance for employees as appropriate. Emotional health and well-being is not covered by law, but most employers would consider they have a duty of care to staff to support and enhance emotional health and well-being and avoid and discourage bullying, stress and disharmony.

This is not a comprehensive list but aims to highlight the care required by law for adult employees (DoH, 2004). In schools, the employees are usually and appropriately considered to be the teaching and ancillary staff. This is particularly relevant when discussing the health promoting school as it is clearly important to promote the health and well-being of not just the pupils, but also the staff employed within the school.

The law relating to promoting health for pupils

Common law principles apply to school pupils' health and safety, with staff being considered *in loco parentis* to the pupils in their charge, i.e. standing in on behalf of the parents and carers. Common law principles are effectively non-statutory guidelines which may or may not be observed by the school. They are generally used and applied in terms of the behavioural and supervisory elements of practice (Stock, 1993).

The legislative framework which is applicable to the health and safety of pupils in school is the Education (School Premises) Regulations 1999. The Regulations state that 'every part of a school building shall be of such design and construction that the safe escape of occupants in case of fire and their health and safety in other respects is reasonably assured (s. 24)'. The Regulations also provide minimum standards for school premises relating to the number of toilets and washbasins per pupil, heating and lighting, and the provision of drinking water.

With regard to the number of toilets and washbasins required under the legislation, there must be one toilet and washbasin per ten children under the age of 5, and one for every 20 children over the age of 5. When the school has children over the age of 8, and has mixed-gender pupils attending, there must be at least two separate rooms available. So, for a school with 90 pupils in Years R–2, as well as ten pupils in Early Years, there should be at least six toilets and washbasins available. Separate facilities must be provided for staff.

Every school, under the Regulations, is required to provide separate space for staff to work in, as well as space for staff to rest and socialise in, but this is not a requirement for pupils.

School as a student's workplace

It has been suggested that school can be viewed in two ways. Firstly, it is a preparation area for life in terms of educational attainment and information, understanding social norms and contexts of the individual within that society, and informing and instructing children as to the expectations and social norms of community participation. Secondly, school can be viewed as a place of occupation. Attendance at school is in the UK considered the sole occupation and, therefore, 'work' of a child.

Typically, children in the UK spend 35 hours per week at school, a similar amount of time to the adult standard working week of 37.5 hours. The current UK health and safety legislative framework is not currently applicable to children in school, but is applicable to the teaching and ancillary adult staff.

This means in practice that staff will undergo ergonomic assessments but children using computers will not, and that staff must have provision for drinks and storage of food but children do not, leading to lunches (often including yoghurts, etc.) being kept at room temperature for several hours prior to consumption (Stock, 1993; Croghan and Johnson, 2003; see also Education (School Premises) Regulations 1999).

Applying the legal context to a health promoting school

The Health and Safety Commission (HSC) has produced a ten-year strategy for occupational health improvement (HSC, 2002). This framework could equally be applied to improving the health of pupils in schools. The targets which have been set are:

- to reduce the number of days lost through sickness absence by 30 per cent by 2010;
- to reduce the incidence of fatal and major injury accidents by 10 per cent by 2010;
- to reduce the incidence of work/occupation related ill health by 20 per cent by 2010.

The strategy explicitly states that health and safety for children should be provided in schools and goes on to state that innovative responses are needed which can be implemented through partnership working.

So, if we are to consider that school is a child's workplace as it is their occupation to attend school, we need to plan effective and innovative mechanisms for increasing their rights as 'workers' so that guidance is not just adhered to but exceeded wherever possible to benefit the pupils' health now and in the future.

Specifically, the NHSP has standards which relate to health and safety:

- The school has an identified health and safety representative and regularly conducts risk assessments.
- Members of the whole school community are aware of their roles and responsibilities in ensuring that the school is a healthy and safe environment which includes addressing child protection issues through the curriculum and having clearly defined procedures for responding to incidents.
- The school provides opportunities for all pupils to develop health skills in relation to first aid.
- The school provides a healthy and safe playground which addresses issues of sun safety, has a quiet area and lunchtime supervisors trained in dealing with bullying and organising play activities.

- The school encourages its staff and pupils to consider cycling and walking to and from school and provides training in safety and security supported by safer travel policies.

(DoH, 2005a)

What does this mean for me

How can I use this to help my school action plan?

In any plans, then, we can consider these outcomes as major aims in supporting the health of pupils, staff and the wider community related to school and use the following three targets to underpin health promotion strategies.

- You can use a measure of current sickness absence both in staff and pupils as a baseline to assess how effective your interventions are.

- You can use an accident book to record any staff or pupil accidents and then use this as a baseline upon which to plan activities.

- Finally, you can assess the reasons for absence as a baseline measure and use this to inform your plan of health promotion activity. For example, if staff are predominantly having time off work due to minor infections such as coughs and colds, you can use this to support a strategy for educating pupils and staff about the spread of infectious disease.

Case study

St Thomas Christopher school invited the local St John Ambulance in to teach children basic first aid in Years 5 and 6, at the request of some of the children. The pupils were then able to receive an award for their personal folders.

These pupils were then given responsibility for monitoring the accident book each week and creating bar charts of the most common accidents. These bar charts were shown to other pupils and discussed during an assembly and were then used to inform changes in play supervision.

Case study

Lady Charlotte's Primary school delivered a questionnaire to all pupils and parents concerning travel to and from school. Many people were using cars despite living within half a mile of the school because of perceptions of danger from the many cars around the school. For one week, everyone was asked to walk if at all possible and cars were restricted from a quarter mile area surrounding the school. The school council pupils drew maps and supplied them through the school to all pupils. Walking buses, staffed by a combination of school staff, parents and governors, were set up to trial for the week. The local community police officer was present as was the crossing patrol staff.

Parents and pupils were surveyed at the end of the week and the walking bus became an integral part of the school travel plan.

Risks to physical health in childhood

Authorised absence rates in England and Wales have remained fairly stable over the last few years at around 5 per cent (DoH, 2005b). This figure relates to all authorised absence, that is absence which has been reported to the school by a parent or carer and for which an explanation has been received which satisfies the school. Although it is not possible to define how much of this is due to pre-agreed family holidays and how much is due to the sickness absence, it can be assumed that a high proportion of this is due to the latter. Estimates suggest around 1–2 per cent of authorised absences are for family holidays, leaving around 3–4 per cent of all authorised absence in primary schools being due to sickness absence (Wardle, 2005).

Individual schools keep account of their own sickness absence rates among pupils and this can be one way of evaluating the efficacy of any interventions with the pupils and their families.

The main causes of sickness absence in the 3–11 year old age range are:

- infectious diseases;

- accidents, burns and accidental poisoning;

- submersion/drowning in water (domestic baths and swimming pools);

- infectious diseases (DoH, 2005b).

The United States Center for Disease Control and Prevention (US CDC, 1998) has estimated that the average school-aged child missed approximately one week annually due to illness-related absenteeism in 1995. The most common infections transmitted in school environments are respiratory and diarrhoeal illnesses. Most of the infections occur at a constant low level but occasionally outbreaks do occur resulting in increased absenteeism. Hand-to-hand contact is the primary mechanism of transmission of these illnesses, and proper hand hygiene techniques have been endorsed as the first defence for reducing the risk of transmission. Most infectious diseases are spread through the close contact of children in schools.

Preventing the spread of infections is an important function for schools because of the impact on the school of an outbreak of an infectious disease. An outbreak of any of these – not usually serious but often debilitating – infections often results in teacher and ancillary staff absence, parental absence from work (due to taking time to care for the sick child), which can increase financial pressures and inequalities and pupil absence (this is particularly damaging in formative environments such as Early Years, when initial socialisation into the group dynamics are taking place). Often these outbreaks can take a long time to dissipate, due to continued reinfection, or to a wide period of the disease organism infecting new people. Routine hand washing with soap and water has been cited by the World Health Organisation (WHO) as being 'the most important hygiene measure in preventing the spread of infection' (US CDC, 1998).

Teaching children to wash their hands and to blow their noses on paper tissues once prior to throwing them away is a key activity for the promotion of health in young children. Learning the appropriate times for hand washing, and learning how and why to undertake this activity needs to be built into the Early Years curriculum, but in a school where this has not happened, care also needs to be taken to ensure that this learning is promoted throughout the school.

What does this mean for me

How can I use this to help my school action plan?

Firstly, you need to assess how much of a problem this is in your school. If sickness absence through minor infectious disease is an issue which you could potentially reduce, then use the lesson plan provided later in the book to educate and inform pupils. You can then measure the impact by assessing future like-for-like seasonal sickness absence (e.g. comparing absence rates in the winter term in the year before activity and in the winter term the following year after the activity). Partnerships which may be helpful in controlling the spread of minor infectious diseases to promote health may include:

● *the school nurse and the local GP* – who can alert you to an outbreak;

● *parents* – who can alert you to an outbreak and who can be involved in supporting your work at home, and who can also decide whether to send a child to school or not;

● *pupils* – who can reinforce peer behaviour and encourage their peers to wash hands, not come to school when ill, etc.;

● *education and teaching staff* – who can also reinforce behavioural patterns of handwashing, nose blowing and not coming to school when ill.

Case study

St Katie's School developed lesson plans relating to hand washing and nose blowing in conjunction with the school nurse and health visitor, specifically aimed at Early Years and Reception.

Sickness absence rates fell significantly and the pupils' attitude, knowledge and behaviour changed. The school nurse undertook a questionnaire survey prior to and three months following the subject lessons with children and families.

The Early Years pupils presented their work to the whole school in an assembly, which was reinforced by pupils' posters being placed in school toilets and in all classrooms, accompanied by boxes of paper tissues.

Accidents

Around half of all accidents involving bicycles which led to hospitalisation in England and Wales in 2004 were seen in those aged under 11 (DoH, 2005b). These range from falling from a bicycle to serious collisions with motorised vehicles including cars, motorcycles and buses (DoH, 2005b). Accidents with fireworks, in the house and in the school, also account for high levels of hospitalisation. Less serious accidents which do not result in hospitalisation are a frequent occurrence in this age group and there is a need for education to raise awareness and skills to avoid such injuries. The school environment is one in which accidents frequently occur: 6,245 children were hospitalised after accidents involving school play equipment in 2004 (DoH, 2005b). The school governors will have a health and safety committee who should be informed if accidents occur with particular items of playground equipment so that policies and procedures can be reviewed.

What does this mean for me?

How can it help my school action plan?

An understanding of how serious a problem this is for your school environment can be achieved in a number of ways. Firstly, the local health visitor (for children under 5) and the local school nurse should be informed whenever a child on their caseload visits Accident and Emergency (A&E) departments. This record usually includes the reason for the child's visit, whether the child was admitted or not and any follow-up information. This allows the nurse or health visitor to identify trends, particularly relating to accidental injuries, which can inform school health promotion activities. Secondly, every school has an accident book in which all accidents should be recorded. Working together with partners such as the local health workers, the chair of the health and safety governors' committee and the lead lunchtime or playground supervisor, this book should be reviewed on a termly basis to identify any recurrent themes. *Every Child Matters* (see website) encourages information sharing between organisations; however, there are some barriers to this such as patient confidentiality, but wherever possible information sharing about individuals can be used together with the information from the hospital attendance slips given to the school nurse or health visitor. These can be combined and collated using the table provided in Resource 2.1.

Submersion/drowning in water

Although this is in reality a subsection of accidents and rarely occurs on primary school grounds (usually involving domestic baths or swimming pools), it is an important cause of harm and hospitalisation in primary aged children. It may not be within the school's power to offer swimming lessons to pupils, but wherever possible schools can work with partners in local authorities and parents or carers to identify and support cheap and accessible swimming lessons in the locality and refer to these termly in newsletters.

What does this mean for me?

How can it help my school action plan?

Providing information and increasing knowledge as to the dangers of unsupervised bathing for parents and children is an area where schools can work together with parents and carers, perhaps inviting in an outside speaker prior to key holiday times. The local fire service or RoSPA (Royal Society for the Prevention of Accidents) may be willing to come and talk to the school and parents.

The following websites, although not a complete list of all which are available, are useful and informative sites with activities and information for children, carers and families.

- http://www.direct.gov.uk
- http://www.lifeguardsupport.co.uk/index.php
- http://www.fireservice.co.uk/safety/watersafety.php
- http://www.rospa.com/waterandleisuresafety
- http://www.nationalwatersafety.org.uk

Item	Number of occurrences this term (accident book)	Number of occurrences this term (A&E slips)	Action to be taken	Lead	Date for review

Other physical health issues

Other risks to children's health relate mainly to the promotion of a healthy lifestyle and include:

- obesity prevention and management and the promotion of healthy diets;
- increasing the desire and opportunity to drink water;
- increasing physical activity opportunities.

Obesity prevention and management and the promotion of healthy diets

Obesity is the condition of being significantly over the ideal weight for height ratio, which increases the risk of serious health implications. Obesity in childhood matters because children who are obese or very overweight are likely to go on to be obese as adults, with the serious health and social consequences which this entails. The main childhood effects of obesity are:

- the psychosocial effects (bullying, low self-esteem, etc.);
- joint and back problems;
- early puberty and therefore reduced adult height;
- diabetes (type 2). (This is a form of diabetes where the body develops insulin resistance and was until recently relatively uncomon in childhood. Type 1 diabetes, on the other hand, is caused by a defect in the immune system and was much more commonly seen in childhood. Type 1 diabetes is not affected by being overweight or obesity; on the other hand, type 2 diabetes is usually seen in children who are overweight or obese.)

Over a quarter of all children aged 2–11 are overweight and around 14 per cent of children in this age group are defined as obese (Wardle, 2005). Some children are more at risk of becoming obese than others. The main factors which raise the child's risk are:

- coming from a poorer family background;
- having parents or carers with a high BMI (Body Mass Index – a measure based on height/weight ratio, which determines weight category);
- living in a deprived area;
- living in an inner-city area;
- being aged 6–10 (Wardle, 2005).

There are occasionally physical causes of obesity such as Prada Willi syndrome, Cushing's disease and others, but this is unusual. The most common cause is taking in more calories than are used by the body, either in growth and daily activities or in physical activity.

Only around one in eight children eats the recommended daily amount of fruit and vegetables (five portions) (Wardle, 2005).

What does this mean for me?

How can it help my school action plan?

The National Healthy Schools standard relating to healthy eating states:

- The school should present consistent, informed messages about healthy eating; for example, the food on offer in vending machines, tuck shops and school meals should complement the taught curriculum.

- The school should provide, promote and monitor healthier food at lunch and break times and in any breakfast clubs where they are provided.

- The school should include education on healthier eating and basic food safety practices in the taught curriculum.

An interdepartmental UK target has been set to halt the year-on-year rise in obesity among those under 11 (HM Treasury, 2004). This will require partnership working and a key element of this relates to schools. All LA maintained schools offer a free portion of fruit to pupils aged between 4 and 7. Often the uptake of this is not monitored and parents are not aware of the type of fruit being offered. Schools could inform parents and carers of the fruit opportunities available in the following week and could provide a recipe a week in the school newsletter. Using one of the pieces of fruit available each week as a tool for teaching could be considered in an assembly.

Extended schools are a particular opportunity for health promotion, especially in relation to activities such as a cookery club, breakfast or other meal club and other activities which will meet the needs of both schools and pupils.

Increasing the desire and opportunity to drink water

Most children do not choose water as their primary drink of choice. However, drinking plenty of water regularly throughout the day can protect health and contribute to well-being. It can also help prevent a range of short- and long-term health problems from headaches and bladder, kidney and bowel problems to cancer. For schools, increasing the water intake of children matters because with dehydration, mental performance deteriorates by 10 per cent, and children have increased thirst, tiredness and irritability. Other drinks contain sugar, which causes sharp energy and mood swings and decreases concentration. Sugar is associated in childhood with panic attacks, nightmares, hyperactivity and behavioural difficulties (Wolraich et al., 1996). It is also associated with increased risk of being overweight and obesity in children and develops a palate in children for lifelong use of sweetened drinks, with little, detrimental or no nutritional value.

What does this mean for me?

How can it help my school action plan?

Children learn better when they are fully hydrated. There are health and safety, public health and health promotion rationales for providing safe, clean and well accepted opportunities for drinking water throughout the day. It demonstrates a commitment to the NHSP and HPS principles concerning healthful environments and opportunities for pupils and staff.

Assembly

Teacher notes

Aims: For the pupils to understand the health benefits of eating a piece of fruit each day.

Resources: One item of the week's fruit

Activities: Children enter to *Food, Glorious Food*
Song/hymn relating to fruits and food
Show children the fruit:

- What could you use it for?
- How many ways could you eat it?
- How could you make it tastier?
- How could you make it less/more healthy?
- What recipe could it be included in?
- Who likes it? How many do you need for one portion of fruit?
- Where does it come from?

Prayer (if appropriate/applicable to setting):

Thank you for the fruits and vegetables that we have to eat. Thank you for the (chosen fruit) which we like to eat. Thank you for giving us (fruit) to help us keep ourselves healthy. We will thank you by eating and enjoying our (fruit) this week. Amen.

Schools should offer children constant opportunities to drink water, including wherever possible carrying individual bottles of water which can stay with the child at all times during the day. This also reduces the child needing to leave the classroom to access drinks.

Increasing physical activity opportunities

Current guidelines suggest that children in the primary age group should be undertaking at least one hour per day of quality physical activity. Most British children do not achieve this – on average, children in the primary age group achieve around half an hour per day. A study by Sport England (Row and Champion, 1999) suggests that over a third of children in primary schools are provided with one hour of PE interventions in school per week, and many children do not have access to other sports or activity facilities. There is good evidence to suggest that increasing any form of physical activity achieves an increase in self-esteem and psychological well-being, physical health and social health through team activities.

What does this mean for me?

How can it help my school action plan?

The NHSP Standards relating to physical activity are as follows.

- The school has a whole-school approach to the promotion of physical activity.

- The school offers all pupils, whatever their age or ability, a minimum of two hours of physical activity a week within and outside the National Curriculum.

- The school is aware of a range of relevant initiatives and networks and takes advantage of appropriate opportunities to promote and develop physical activity.

- The school encourages its staff, pupils, parents/carers and other adults, for example, sports development officers, to become involved in promoting physical activity and develops their skills, abilities and understanding through appropriate training.

Again, working with partners such as the local health care providers, who often have a physical activity lead, and with local councils, schools can be a key facilitator for children to access physical activity, by providing and reinforcing information for children, parents and carers about local facilities, clubs, etc. Schools can also provide educational opportunities as to the importance of physical activity and what constitutes an active half hour.

Schools could develop, in partnership with pupils, parents and the wider local community, a school travel plan which offers physical activity, such as walking buses or school bicycle clubs. This is a key contributory factor to a healthy schools award.

Case study

Colin Wood Primary School began offering once-weekly after-school activities for Year 3 pupils. All activities had an element of physical activity as a focus, and were voluntary. Options included disco dancing, country dancing, football, short tennis and yoga. Each session lasted for 45 minutes. The pupils told younger pupils about the sessions in assemblies and created a social desire for such activities among younger children. These were then offered to Year 1 and Year 2 pupils to access on a weekly basis.

Other issues

Apart from risks to physical health, children in the primary age group also need education and support around:

- sex and relationship education (SRE);
- understanding and information about smoking and avoiding pressure to smoke – including a smoke-free policy;
- understanding and information about drugs and avoiding pressure to take drugs or alcohol;
- sun safe activities and information.

Each of these needs to be undertaken in a sensitive and age-appropriate way, which will be considered in the following chapters relating to specific age groups.

What does this mean for me?

How can it help my school action plan?

NHSP Standards for these areas include:

SRE

- The school has a policy which is owned and implemented by all members of the school including pupils and parents, and which is delivered in partnership with local health and support services.

- The school has a planned sex and relationships education programme (including information, social skills development and values clarification) which identifies learning outcomes, appropriate to pupils' age, ability, gender and level of maturity and which is based on pupils' needs assessment and a knowledge of vulnerable pupils.

- Staff have a sound basic knowledge of sex and relationships issues and are confident in their skills to teach sex education and discuss sex and relationships.

- Staff have an understanding of the role of schools in contributing to the reduction of unwanted teenage conceptions and the promotion of sexual health.

Smoking and drugs (including alcohol)

- The school has a named member of staff and a governor who are responsible for drug education provision.

- The school has a planned drug education programme involving development of skills, starting from early years, which identifies learning outcomes, appropriate to pupils' ages, ability and level of maturity and which is based on pupils' needs assessment.

- The school has a policy, owned and implemented by the whole school, including parents/carers, for managing drug-related incidents which includes identifying sources of support for pupils and alternatives to exclusion.

- Staff understand the role that schools can play in the national drug strategy and are confident to discuss drugs issues and services with pupils.

- The school works with the police, youth service and local drug services in line with the Drug Action Team strategy to develop its understanding of local issues and to inform its policy.

Conclusions

There are many things which schools can do to address the issues which affect the physical health and well-being of primary school-aged children. The very nature of many of these risks means that the school needs to identify and work with partners in the local community to help children to ultimately spend more of their time healthy and in school. Healthy children are better able to learn and are more likely to achieve their potential.

CHAPTER 3

Promotion of emotional health and well-being in classrooms

Chapter aims

This chapter focuses on how and why to promote emotional health in primary schools and classroom environments, including what to do, the rationale for undertaking the suggested activities and how to evaluate activities in the short and medium term.

What is emotional health?

The National Service Framework (NSF) for Children, Young People and Maternity Services (DoH, 2004b), and Every Child Matters (see website), which are both to be delivered through health, social care and education interfaces and departments, recognise that child and adolescent emotional and mental health is an important area for development across all partner agencies.

Mental health and emotional well-being have been identified as not simply an absence of adverse mental health issues, but are about children who are able to:

- develop emotionally, creatively, intellectually and spiritually;
- initiate, develop and sustain mutually satisfying personal relationships;
- face problems, resolve them and learn from them;
- are confident and assertive;
- are aware of others and empathise with them;
- use and enjoy solitude;
- play and have fun;
- laugh, both at themselves and at the world.

Therefore positive mental health promotion in schools should aim to have each of these as a set of overarching principles and objectives to enable evaluation.

In a large study by the British Department for Education and Skills (DfES, 2004b) only a very small minority of schools were working towards or had met the criteria for providing for pupils' emotional health and well-being. The main barrier identified to schools delivering emotional health promotion was the low level of awareness of the importance of the issue.

Risks to emotional health and well-being in childhood

An Office of National Statistics survey (ONS, 1999) showed that 10 per cent of all children in the UK suffer from mental health problems, with some vulnerable groups particularly affected. It also showed early identification and intervention is essential in achieving positive outcomes for these children.

There are three main vulnerabilities which may increase a child's risk of developing a mental/emotional health disorder:

- *Environmental and societal factors*. These include living in a socio-economically deprived family or area, discrimination, low educational support and experience of a disaster or similar trauma.

- *Family or relationship factors*. These may include witnessing parental conflict, family breakdown, witnessing or being party to hostility or rejection from the family or others, physical, emotional or sexual abuse, a parent or other close person experiencing physical or mental ill health (including addiction, criminality, etc.), disclarity or inconsistency in expectation or discipline and family or others not adapting to the child's changing needs as they physically and emotionally develop. Also in this category is the bereavement or loss of relatives or friends (this may include moving home and loss of friendship).

- *Factors relating to the child*. These include developmental delay or impairment, communication issues, physical illness or problems, genetic predispositions to some health issues, low IQ or academic attainment and some learning disabilities.

Bullying

Bullying can take many forms – emotional, physical or verbal. The term bullying is usually applied when the behaviour takes place on more than one occasion. It is an activity which can have serious consequences in terms of physical, emotional and social damage to the child being bullied. Bullying can also involve new technologies: for example text messaging, e-mailing and instant messaging services have all been reported as tools used in bullying.

Bullying is a potentially very serious issue, with reported cases ending in suicide in several countries. All children have the right to a safe environment and preventing bullying is a core activity to ensure that environments are safe.

Resilience

In childhood, building resilience relates to building the capacity to deal with adversity and unexpected change. A child's resilience is built on internal and external factors and resources.

Internal resilience is based upon the child's innate personality and ability. External resilience is based upon factors which the child has access to or owns. External resilience factors, for example, may be exposure to role models, autonomy and encouragement to try things for themselves, and boundaries which provide safety and access to friends and education. Internal resilience factors, for example, may include communication skills, empathy, problem-solving and self-affection and pride. Building these factors and supporting the enhancement of them is a key element in developing resilience.

Resilience is usually developed through interactions with family and school. Effective strategies for building resilience have been identified and include:

- flexibility in school service provision in accommodating a range of cultural and community actions and behaviours;

- positive experiences and reinforcement of positive behaviours;

- mutually trusting and positive relationships with school staff and peers;

- the development of skills and independence;

- the development and maintenance of attachments;

- help with resolving problems and issues;

- provision of out-of-school care;

- the creation and maintenance of home–school links (Newman, 2004).

What does this mean for me?

How can it help my school action plan?

The NHSP standards relating to the promotion of emotional health (including bullying) are as follows.

- Opportunities are provided for pupils' views to inform policy and practice.

- The school has a policy and code of practice for tackling bullying, which is owned, understood and implemented by all members of the school community and includes contact with external support agencies.

- The school openly addresses issues of emotional health and well-being by enabling pupils to understand what they are feeling and by building their confidence to learn.

- The school identifies and supports the emotional health needs of staff. (DoH, 2005a)

Education and school health staff need to be aware of risk factors so that they can identify children who may be at risk and provide some supportive interventions. It may be necessary to have an INSET or teacher training day led by an outside agency or the local LA to allow for better support and awareness of these issues. Through the Department for Education and Skills (DfES), a new curriculum resource, SEAL (Social and Emotional Aspects of Learning), is available to all schools. It is a curriculum resource to help primary schools develop children's social, emotional and behavioural skills. It includes assemblies and follow-up ideas for work in class and is available to order by contacting dfes@prolog.uk.com

Common disorders

The most commonly seen issues relating to children's mental ill health are as follows:

- *Conduct disorder*: This is seen when children repeatedly break the rules and regulations of a society or community and affects around 10 per cent of children. Children with Attention Deficit Disorder (around 5 per cent of primary school children) are more at risk of this disorder and it usually manifests in young children as 'temper tantrums' and aggression. When a child is suspected of having this disorder, partnerships are needed to ensure it is not simply a reaction to one area of life, as the disorder will prompt this level of behaviour in all circumstances.

- *Anxiety*. Around 10 per cent of primary school children will suffer from excessive anxiety which affects their ability to carry out their daily activities. Starting school is a particularly anxious time for children, especially if they have not been to a preschool or experienced a non-family environment previously. Most children will exhibit some forms of anxious behaviour (clinging to parents for ten minutes, etc.) for anything up to a few weeks after starting school: this is often normal behaviour. Parents are good judges of their child's behaviour, especially at this time. If the anxious behaviour is lasting for a longer period, or the child cannot be distracted, or does not play with other children, this may indicate a child who needs extra support and specialist intervention.

- *Obsessive compulsive behaviour*. This is often linked to anxiety and refers to repeated activities or rituals such as hand washing undertaken by children to provide emotional comfort.

- *Depression*: Around 2 per cent of primary school children suffer with depression. The most common symptoms of this in early childhood are withdrawal from family and friends, moodiness, irritability, sleep and dietary disturbance.

What does this mean for me?

How can it help my school action plan?

Whenever a child is suspected of having a mental health issue, the school should follow the locally defined protocols for accessing help and support for the child and family. The role of the school in identifying mental health issues is that of supportive partner and referrals should be made to specialist mental health services such as CAMHS (Child and Adolescent Mental Health Services). In the case of suspected abuse, local protocols should be followed immediately.

What does this mean for me?

How can it help my school action plan?

Being part of a group or community, such as that inherent in a school or class of pupils, can be a positive mental health experience. However, for everyone in the community to gain, the group has to be inclusive. Therefore, whole-school assemblies are to be encouraged as they engender a sense of belonging to a wider whole. The school can develop a plan of rolling assemblies and activities which specifically promote mental health and can support this with classroom-based activities.

Strategies for group emotional health promotion in primary schools

The main group activities which are used in primary education to promote mental health and emotional well-being are as follows:

- *Circle time*. This is a natural teaching mechanism which centres around sitting in a circle. It is based on equality, openness and honesty. The teacher or leader facilitates rather than formally teaches concepts. The ground rules for circle time should include:
  - one person to speak at a time: perhaps prompted by a prop (such as a stuffed toy, which is passed from pupil to pupil);
  - everyone having the right to choose not to speak if they want;
  - being non-judgemental;
  - everyone having the right to their opinion.

- *Role play*. This is closely linked with drama, and often involves a situational dilemma which the participants (the pupils) must act out and then act out a solution. It may include empathy with someone else.

- *Art and creativity to support emotional well-being*. This refers to the creation of group collages, or group 'happy books' to allow children to feel included.

- *Guided relaxation strategies*. This refers to supporting children in managing anxiety by providing education and examples of guided relaxation, along with deep breathing mechanisms.

Consensus lines

A technique which is often referred to in this book, especially within the lesson plans is the use of a consensus line. This is an imaginary line of agreement, which children are asked to stand on to demonstrate their opinion. This can be adapted to corners of the room. Following initial locations, and discussions of why they are standing on that place, it is useful to ask if anyone wants to move because they have been persuaded by another's argument.

Example consensus line:

Jane	Kara	Sajad	Emily	Asif	Chen	Sam
Louise		Thomas Joseph	Miriam	James Patrick		Natasha

Agree		Not sure		Disagree

Example room-based consensus line:

Agree		Disagree
	Not sure	
Strongly agree		Strongly disagree

Strategies for individual emotional health promotion in primary schools

Individual activities for promoting emotional well-being might include the following:

- discussion of a dilemma or situation – think about how you would feel in this situation;

- emotional literacy and intelligence;

- providing books which have an element of emotional distress or discomfort, then prompting discussion;

- individual art work – drawing a picture of something that provokes an emotional response;

- differentiated teaching.

Assessing emotional difficulties

Some children will be identified by schools, usually in conjunction with the special educational needs coordinator (SENCO) as being at risk of or having some emotional or mental health issues. In the case of any suspected issues being raised, refer these children to the school SENCO. The Code of Practice for Special Educational Needs sets out clear guidance for meeting children's needs, particularly in relation to those children who have emotional and behavioural difficulties. This includes children with mental and emotional health problems. This Code sets out a clear assessment process for children who may need additional support as a result of a range of difficulties.

Involving families and carers and other partners

Helping children to feel part of a wider community, able to cope with life and to know where to go for help, is a key element of promoting feelings of emotional safety and well-being. Involving parents in this health-enhancing partnership will help the child to feel confident that adults are working together in their interests. Explaining to parents and carers what is happening in school and why and providing 'take-home' exercises to promote discussion between children and their carers is helpful in this respect.

Case Study

A school nurse was routinely used to visiting senior schools and delivering an informal 'drop in' session. Pupils aged 11–18, staff and parents were all aware of this and could visit the nurse to discuss any issues without the need for an appointment. The nurse approached school E to deliver a similar scheme as a pilot in the primary school. Letters went out to parents, class visits and assemblies were carried out by the nurse to pupils and all staff were informed. The nurse was present on site from 8.30 a.m. to 10 a.m. once a week. Following a visit from a parent expressing concern about her child, and then a visit from two pupils who were friends with the same child, the nurse was able to identify a child with significant anxiety issues relating to SATs examinations which had prompted behavioural issues.

Conclusions

Promoting emotional and mental health and well-being is central to promoting holistic well-being in children. There are a number of stressors on children, intrinsic to them, extrinsic to them, or environmental – around them – which can prompt episodes of anxiety or emotional distress. Developing an understanding of why we feel as we do is inherent to the development of key life and coping skills to help us to deal with stressors as they arise. This development of resilience is an important skill for all children to be supported with.

CHAPTER 4

Promotion of social health and well-being in classrooms – including citizenship

Chapter aims

This chapter aims to consider why social and community health in school and classroom environments is important. It discusses what it means to be healthy or unhealthy in this respect, with some wider whole-school suggestions for what to do, the rationale for doing the suggested activities and how to evaluate the activities.

What is social health?

Social health lacks a formal definition, but essentially it refers to being able to participate in or influence decisions which affect individuals within the wider context of a group. Being socially healthy, therefore, suggests an individual who is empowered to participate in decisions which affect them. A socially healthy adult in a democratic society has a vote, which they can choose to use or not. A socially healthy child is able to make informed decisions and choices and is aware of the consequences of their actions. They are also aware of the impact on themselves or on those around them. It is often difficult for children to perceive they can effect or influence change. Schools have a role in promoting and empowering children for their childhood. They also, through education and information gathering and sharing, have a role in supporting children to become empowered adults.

A continuing conflict lies at the very heart of social well-being and social health: does being part of a society constrain or empower participants? Societal paradigms suggest that the amalgamation of individuals into wider society negates the power and influence of an individual and enhances the power of society as one whole individual construct to constrain the individuals within it into behaving in a certain societally defined manner. On the other hand, the social action paradigm suggests that society is an abstract construct and that it is individuals whose actions are socially orientated who effect change. Certainly, however, feeling a sense of belonging and having an awareness of societal rules and regulations is a key element of social health. If a socially healthy society is one which looks after, and is supportive of, its members, then this is the aim of social health promotion.

What is community?

Community is a term that describes a group of people or organisations with common interests, characteristics or experiences and a sense of belonging. As such a community could be in the context of a school, a school class, a year group or a whole school, or the school and the surrounding geographical area.

However, simply defining groups of people as a community because they have common characteristics could be considered oversimplistic and paternalistic: indeed this lack of consideration of individual attributes and the forced alignment of groups of people based on one or two common characteristics leads to stereotyping. It is therefore imperative that, firstly, people are given the choice of belonging or not belonging to certain communities wherever possible and that there are multifaceted approaches taken to identifying and linking people to communities.

Applying all this to citizenship

Citizenship has been a core component of the PSHE curriculum since 2002. For primary schools (Key Stages 1 and 2) there is a non-statutory framework for delivery which gives pupils the knowledge, skills and understanding to play an effective role in society.

What does this mean for me?

How can it help my school action plan?

The NHSP Standards relating to citizenship, and therefore social health and well-being, are:

● the school recognises that all aspects of school life can have an impact on the development of pupils in becoming informed, active and responsible citizens.

● the school provides opportunities for pupils to be actively involved in the life of their school and communities. (DoH, 2005a)

The UN Convention on the Rights of the Child states that all children and young people have the right to express their views freely in all matters affecting them. This is a basic human right supported by Every Child Matters (see website), and is one which a socially healthy school environment will promote, whether through the use of school councils, forums, peer mentors or some other mechanism.

Extended schools are a mechanism for encouraging and enhancing community participation with schools and health. Extended schools are schools which work with local providers (and in many cases other schools) to provide access to a core offer of extended services, which may include (see Chapter 1):

- childcare 8 a.m. – 6 p.m., all year round;

- parenting and family support;

- a varied range of activities (study support), including sport and music clubs;

- swift and easy referral to specialist services such as speech therapy and health drop-ins;

- community use of facilities including adult and family learning and ICT.

'Extended school' is not a status that schools centrally apply for as the activities provided depend on the needs of the local community. Schools need to work together with their local authority (in particular the extended schools remodelling adviser), pupils, parents, the local community and local providers to decide how and when services will be provided.

Invoking a sense of in-school community

Four key criteria for achieving a sense of community have been proposed:

- membership/belonging;

- influence/ability to effect change;

- shared values;

- shared emotional connections. (DfEE, 1999)

Therefore we should use these four concepts as the base criteria for any activities which aim to improve or invoke a sense of community to improve the health outcomes and potential of the school community.

Throughout the citizenship strand of the PSHE curriculum, three key elements are noted:

- social and moral responsibility;

- community involvement;

- political literacy.

We also need to consider how these three strands can be incorporated into activities to provide a holistic approach to health and well-being promotion.

Membership/belonging

What does this mean for me?

How can it help my school action plan?

For primary school children, this may be the first opportunity for them to be part of a wider community than their immediate family. The benefits of feeling part of the wider school community can be seen behaviourally in individuals who will alter their behaviour to achieve the goals of the group. It can be seen also in that a sense of belonging makes children feel secure.

Invoking a sense of belonging to a school community often begins with a uniform: at its simplest, this may be a shared colour ('although we don't have a uniform for the children in the Early Years Unit, we do ask that, wherever possible, they wear red jumpers/cardigans or shirts so that they can be easily identified as being from our school Early Years Unit') right through to a full uniform. The use of such a prop to engender a sense of belonging can be enhanced by the school staff frequently commenting on the shared nature of the uniform. Talking about the school as a family often helps engender a sense of togetherness and membership of the school community: it becomes aspirational for younger siblings to wear the uniform colour, for example. A shared and mutually agreed set of school rules and regulations, known as the school code, will also help to quickly establish a sense of community. Other props which enhance this feeling are school and team/house names, colours and groupings.

Influence/ability to effect change

What does this mean for me?

How can it help my school action plan?

This is often seen as problematic for schools with young pupils: how can they influence and effect change? The development of school councils, consisting of pupil representatives voted for by each year or class group, including wherever possible the very youngest members of the school, allows pupils to feel that their contribution to the school is important. It also allows the school a forum for communicating with pupils and understanding the concerns of the pupils in a safe environment. Positive peer leadership develops and the responsibility for maintaining good behaviour is shifted away from teachers and educational staff and towards members of the classroom and in-school community. Pupils can often develop skills to resolve conflicts among their peers and there is some evidence that disruptive behaviour, vandalism, truancy and exclusions reduce (Cremin, 2002).

A second mechanism to enhance pupils' ability to influence and effect change is to set up peer counsellor/mentor networks. In this way, a child starting in Reception is mentored by a child in Year 1. They have regular meetings to enable this to happen: in the first half term every week the two classes can get together; in the following half term every two weeks. This provides the Year 1 child with responsibility for someone with whom they have some empathy and the Reception child is able to be reassured by the child in Year 1. This can continue throughout the school, engendering a sense of community responsibility.

A bullying club works in a similar way but allows children in the final year at school to be trained and support children in the rest of the school by being available at lunchtime or break times.

Theses types of schemes need adult supervision and clear guidance for the mentors/peer supporters to talk to an adult if they feel the need, but can provide good mechanisms for inclusivity from an early age.

Shared values

What does this mean for me?

How can it help my school action plan?

Enhancing shared values in school is strongly linked with aspects which have previously been discussed, such as shared rules or codes, shared uniforms and shared agreement over what is considered to be appropriate behaviour.

Setting classroom rules early in the school year is a practical application of this which encourages a sense of belonging and enforces social norms while allowing the pupils to influence change.

Shared emotional connections

What does this mean for me?

How can it help my school action plan?

The sense of shared emotional connections and bonds can be enhanced through group-level activities, the school participating in a competition, the school working together as a team and inter-house groups playing against each other on sports day. It can also be engendered through evocation of past events relating to the school and to the teachers; this will help to create a bond between pupils and teachers.

Group decisions around the school code and school rules are helpful at creating emotional bonds, and ensuring public praise whenever things go particularly well will also engender this sense. Using paired discussions and paired/shared outcome development is also a helpful tool for eliciting emotional connections.

Working with the wider school community

The 'wider school community' refers to the other people or agencies with a direct stakeholder interest in what happens at school. The underlying sociological context of empowering stakeholders in potentially disempowered communities to take responsibility for their own community needs and to regulate the acceptability of what happens within the community has informed the development of community level approaches from a wider responsibility agenda.

This ultimately relates to offering communities the skills, power and knowledge to effect change in their community. The overarching aim is to decrease the top-down authoritative and increase a bottom-up approach to influencing and effecting change.

In the case of the primary school, the wider school community stakeholders may include parents, carers, grandparents, siblings and other schools with a connection to the school (e.g. feeder or receiver schools). Involving these groups will help the wider school family to participate and feel involved in their child's education. Ultimately, this can lead to increased compliance with school requests for support.

Membership/belonging for the wider community

What does this mean for me?

How can it help my school action plan?

To help establish a sense of membership and belonging for the wider school community participants, these stakeholders need to be supported and asked to participate in the school on a regular basis. Inviting parents/grandparents/carers into school twice a year to help out with their child will increase their understanding of the school's aims and objectives, and will increase their feeling that they belong to the wider school community. Having a weekly newsletter with not only practical information but also other information in it helps to support this feeling.

Extended schools have a major role to play in this area. Whether your school is planning to become or is already an extended school, or is working together with another local extended school, this can be used within your planning to ensure the widest sense of community involvement.

Influence/ability to effect change for the wider community

What does this mean for me?

How can it help my school action plan?

Often the wider school community is not invited to participate in decision making or does not feel that their opinions matter. Using the biannual parents/grandparents/carers day as a forum to ask for opinions about issues relating to the school is a useful way to allow these stakeholders to feel included.

Following the example set by the large chain supermarkets and providing a feedback newsletter after these meetings will help stakeholders see how they have influenced change (see example newsletter).

Example School Newsletter

Team of the week:

Red: 120 house points!!
CONGRATULATIONS

Star pupil of the week:

Bob Bobbins
For helping a friend in need
Well done Bob!

CLASS of the week:
R1a: For very Good behaviour on their trip to the Post Office
Good work 1a!

Carer of the week:
Mrs Jones (George's grandma)
For helping Class 2 by sending in some photos
Thank you!

Stuartville School Community News

Dear Friends,

Welcome to Stuartville Community News

We (all the children, the teachers and staff) would like to thank all the parents, grandparents, brothers and sisters who came to our second biannual school sharing day. We had a great time showing you all our hard work, and we really enjoyed having you all here, especially sharing lunchtime together!

You may remember that in the afternoon, we asked you to complete some information sheets for us and we had a chat about how you felt we as a school were doing. Here is a summary of what you said and what we plan to do to make sure we are supporting you and your children as much as possible.

You said . . .
We will . . .

You said . . .
We will . . .

You said . . .
We will . . .

Please remember that if you have any other comments you can always come and chat to us, talk to your class teacher or write them in the home–school communication book.

As always, the carer of the week was nominated by pupils. A pupil of the week was also nominated by pupils. If you would like to nominate a pupil or a carer, please talk to your class teacher.

Example Home–School Contract

Pupil name:

Class:

I will work hard to do my best at Stuartville School by:

> Being kind and helpful
> Listening to my teacher and my carer
> Working hard
> Having fun!

Signed:

Picture of me:

Parent/carer name:

I will support   to achieve their potential at Stuartville School by:

> Reading the home–school diary each week and signing to show I have read it, giving my comments when necessary
> Listening to them read each night for 15 minutes
> Asking them about their day at school, and telling them about mine
> Telling the class teacher if I have any concerns

Signed:

Class teacher:

I will support   to achieve their potential at Stuartville School by:

> Reading the home–school diary each week and signing to show I have read it, giving my comments each week
> Listening to them read each day for 15 minutes
> Telling the carer if I have any concerns

Signed:

Shared values for the wider community

What does this mean for me?

How can it help my school action plan?

Offering parents/carers a contract when their child starts school which allows them to agree to participate in the shared values of the school will help the stakeholders to feel part of the wider school community (see example contract). Sections 110 and 111 of the School Standards and Framework Act 1998 state that all schools must have a home–school agreement, which forms the basis of a communication between school and home offering shared values and expectations of school, pupils and parents. It may be possible to tie the two issues together by incorporating the ideals of the example contract into your home–school agreement (HSA).

Asking the pupil to sign or draw a picture of themselves on the contract will also enhance its utility and sense of shared importance.

Shared emotional connections with the wider community

What does this mean for me?

How can it help my school action plan?

The use of a biannual get-together (teacher and parent/pupil events), the newsletters and the contracts should help to encourage this process. Clearly stating in the school prospectus that there is an ethos of shared emotional bonds between wider school community members and the in-school community of teachers and pupils helps these stakeholders feel more participatory towards the school. Other options to involve the wider community are intergenerational groups, parent groups and other users of facilities in the school (such as ICT suites).

Working with the wider external community

What does this mean for me?

How can it help my school action plan?

A sense of social health and well-being cannot happen in isolation from the wider community who may not participate in the day-to-day activities of the school but who may have influence on or be influenced by the school and its pupils.

Ensuring that pupils are aware of the wider community perspective will help them to be able to understand the wider constructs of society. Inviting these community members into school at least once a year establishes these relationships and the importance of different areas of society working together.

For example, once a year:

- Around the time of Armistice Day, invite some members of the local British Legion in to talk to the children about their lives now and what their childhoods were like.

- Invite the local MP and local councillors to talk to children about politics and democracy.

- Have a community day and ask local representatives of the local community, shop-keepers, religious and cultural leaders, and local councillors to come in and share a day of learning.

- Have a people who help us day and invite firefighters, nurses, dentists, crossing patrol people, police representatives, etc.

- Have a cultural day, with representatives from the cultures living around the school available to talk about similarities between cultures.

- Also perhaps offer the weekly newsletter to friends of the school via e-mail or post so that the wider community remains involved and included in school life.

CHAPTER 5

Partnership working to promote health

Chapter aims

This chapter focuses on who can and should work together and what different professionals can do to support each other. It also covers the roles and responsibilities of different child education, health and social care professionals. The evidence about working in partnerships and how to evaluate partnership working is also explored.

How can the school work with others to promote health?

As has been identified previously, interdepartmental guidance published as the National Service Framework for Children, Young People and Maternity Services (DoH, 2004b), and Every Child Matters (see website) demonstrate that improving education, health and social care outcomes is not the sole responsibility of one agency, nor can one agency work in isolation to achieve all of the welfare goals for any individual child. The school should be a major partner in all partnerships to support children and their families to achieve their potential. In the UK, the development of a shared qualification in Personal, Social and Health Education (PSHE) for both teachers and nursing staff is a move forward; however, more understanding of the roles of other professionals in promoting the health and well-being of children can only be achieved if there is increased shared educational opportunities for staff as this aids the understanding of the roles and responsibilities of other professionals. The most obvious barrier to collaborative working practice, apart from a lack of understanding of roles and responsibilities, is the differing political and professional agendas of education and healthcare workers. However, schools have been identified as key settings in which to improve health and to reduce health inequalities (DfEE, 1999) in partnership with multiple agencies.

> **Case study**
>
> ## People Who Help Us Day at Charles Lane School
>
> Following on from a topic being studied within Year 1 combined with a parent participating in a fundraising sports event, the school held a 'People Who Help Us' day. Children were able to dress up as people who help us and were asked to describe who they were and why they had chosen that person. At lunchtime, local service providers were invited in (the school nurse, the local GP, the local dental nurse, a community fireman, a community policeman, the crossing patrol wardens), the invitations having been created and sent by the children who served lunch to the service providers. In the afternoon family members were invited in to school to participate in classroom-based activities, and the parent engaged in fundraising was asked to talk to the children about his activities and rationale for doing them.
>
> The children reflected on the day afterwards and wrote a newspaper describing the day, which was circulated widely.

The principles of wider community participatory approaches to facilitate community involvement and development are:

- *Participation* – equal voices for all interested and implicated parties.

- *Collaboration and partnership* – recognition that existing community structures, organisations or groups can improve community health.

- *Equality and equity* – that everyone has the right to equal access to health promotion and protecting resources, and that they should be implemented where there are deficits.

- *Collective action* – bringing people and organisations together to discuss and deal with local needs.

- *Empowerment* – allowing individuals, organisations and communities to gain control over their lives and activities.

Community participatory approaches can help build and release existing capacity within the school and surrounding communities.

The 'ladder of participation' (Arnstein, 1969) demonstrates and categorises how institutions generally use citizen participation methods based on both societal and individual motive and effectiveness (see Table 5.1). The least effective levels to effect change include manipulation and education where it is assumed that an action has public support simply by the lack of substantial opposition. At these levels, no real effort is made to inform the public objectively. The second tier involves forms of 'tokenism' such as informing and consultation where more of an effort is made to tell the public about future actions, but the underlying power lies within the traditional power holder (the health professional, government, etc.) to make the decisions. Finally there are the most effective levels of representation, which include partnership, delegated power and citizen control. At these levels, there is exchange and delegation of power through negotiation and consensus building.

Table 5.1 Levels of engagement

Level of involvement and participation	Type of involvement or participation	Activity to describe the level
1	Manipulation	These assume a passive audience who
2	Education	are given what may be partial or constructed information.
3	Information	People are informed as to what is going to happen, what is happening or what has happened.
4	Consultation	People are given a voice without power to make a difference.
5	Involvement	People's views have some influence, but traditional power holders continue to make the final decisions.
6	Partnership	People begin to negotiate with power holders, and may be involved in agreeing terms of reference and responsibilities.
7	Delegated power	Some power is delegated.
8	Citizen control	All power is delegated.

Adapted from Arnstein (1969).

Partners and their roles

This is not a comprehensive list of all possible partners but aims to give an idea of the roles/responsibilities relating to health promotion, and how to engage them in health promotion in your school.

Education partners

Education partners can be engaged through the potential delivery of DfES targets. Educational attainment is related to positive health, for example, and therefore schools with a sound health promotion policy and delivery structure are likely to see an improvement in educational attainment.

Headteacher

A headteacher is a qualified teacher who leads a team of teaching and non-teaching staff and has overall delegated responsibility for the day-to-day management of the school and for curriculum development and delivery. The headteacher can be the lead professional for the school health promotion plan and can apply for healthy schools awards and other awards or schemes supporting and supported by the school health promotion plan and associated activities.

Educational psychologist

Educational psychologists are qualified psychologists who work in schools and district area offices aiming to resolve children's learning and behaviour problems, especially those related to child devlopment. Psychological methods are used to study the development of motivation, instruction, assessment and other related issues influencing the interaction between teaching and learning.

Class teacher

Every class of pupils has a qualified teacher, except for pre-school units which are often taught by those with with NNEB (National Nursery Examination Board) qualifications or the equivalent under the supervision of the Early Years teacher. The class teacher has to develop the students' learning in a positive way through planning, evaluating and delivering lessons within the curriculum frameworks provided within the guidelines of the DfES. They are often helped by classroom assistants who work with the teacher as a team to support the children in the class.

Cook

The school cook has responsibility for the safe and hygienic delivery of food to children in schools. S/he can be engaged through the HSE legislative framework described in earlier chapters to support health promotion activities. Being involved from an early stage is also likely to increase engagement with activities and the school action plan.

Lunchtime supervisors

Lunchtime supervisors are responsible for the safety, security and good behaviour of pupils during lunchtime and sometimes through daytime playtime. This means they are in an ideal position to observe children's behaviour and eating habits and to encourage positive physical, emotional and social well-being. As with the school cook, supervisors can be engaged through the HSE legislative framework described in earlier chapters to support health promotion activities. Being involved from an early stage is also likely to increase engagement with activities and the school action plan.

Crossing patrol staff

Crossing patrol staff are employed by the LA to police the crossing of roads. Again they are in an ideal position to support and encourage healthier behaviour and may again be engaged through the HSE legislative framework described in earlier chapters to support health promotion activities. Being involved from an early stage is also likely to increase engagement with activities and the school action plan.

The governing body

School governors form the largest volunteer workforce in the UK with around 350,000 people fulfilling this role. The governing body is chaired by a nominated volunteer from the governing body (chair of governors). The governing body of the school is the management body and must ensure that school staff and premises comply with the LA health and safety policies and practices. In foundation schools, the governing body is considered the employer, with the responsibilities described earlier.

The governing body has to have a minimum of two committees: finance and premises, and personnel. Health and safety may be a stand-alone committee, but may be incorporated into the finance and premises committee. As previously described, most of the responsibilities relate to employee welfare, but the governing body must have its own policies for pupil health care, such as support for children with medical needs in school, child protection and other related health issues.

The governors also decide the school SRE policy. For this reason, they should be involved in the school health promotion plan and the legislative frameworks again support their engagement. It is also possible for schools to apply for project and other funding relating to health promotion and other positive and creative projects which enhance both the school environment and the school's position.

Health sector partners

Health sector partners can be engaged as key partners in the health promotion plan of the school through the local primary care organisation, which has Department of Health targets to achieve relating to the public health of school children, in particular halting the year-on-year rise in obesity in 11-year-old children and reducing the prevalence of smoking among children. There are also Department for Culture, Media and Sport and HM Treasury targets relating to the amount of physical activity undertaken by school children. Local primary care organisations can be engaged to work as partners with schools to help in both baseline and follow-up assessment to allow them to demonstrate the achievement of these targets.

School health nurse

The school health nurse must be a qualified general nurse who may have completed other training to become a qualified Registered Specialist Public Health Nurse (School Nursing). The school health nurse provides and is responsible for holistic health support for school-aged children and their families. They are often situated in local health centres and visit schools on a regular basis. They are able to provide health education and health promotion as part of their general remit.

Health visitor

A health visitor is a qualified or registered nurse who has undertaken further training so that they can work as part of the primary health care team. Their role is to promote health and the prevention of illness.

School doctor

The school doctor is a medical doctor working in the community particularly with children of school age, assessing medical problems which affect schooling.

School dentist

The school dentist is a community dentist who visits the school at regular intervals to assess the oral hygiene of the children in primary schools.

Physical activity lead

This is a worker often employed by the local health care provider and/or the local council who is responsible for ensuring that children meet and maintain the chosen health target of 30 minutes' exercise every day, through providing and organising events to promote exercise in children.

Local authority sector

The local authority needs to be engaged because the work in configuration with schools will contribute towards the achievement of their goals and targets. For example, all schools should have active travel plans by 2010, and this cannot be achieved unless authorities work in partnership with schools.

Trading Standards

Trading Standards provide a consumer education service in schools and community groups. They can be contacted through your local authority.

Transport and the Environment Department

The Transport and Environment Department works alongside the Department of Health and the government to produce travel plans through the Choosing Health initiative, which aims to increase the number of children who walk or cycle to school.

Home partners

There are varying levels of engagement which allow home partners to engage with the school community. It will be very difficult to engage with partners if the level of engagement is not at least 5 (see Table 5.1 earlier), allowing the home partners some level of influence. Without this, or without a perception that their voice is able to achieve change, partners will very quickly disengage.

Parent/carer

The role of the parent and carer is to ensure pupil attendance and to support and provide guidance and encouragement for pupils' further home study. The parent/carer needs to establish clear communication between themselves and the school to ensure the child's health and well-being.

Pupil

The role of the pupil is to attend school and contribute to the best of their ability in lessons, as part of the school community, working alongside teachers to enable them to get the best out of each other.

PSHE certification

The PSHE certification programme for school nurses and teachers has been adapted from the Teachers Standards framework and allows those who teach PSHE to study for and receive a multidisciplinary qualification. It consists of a core element (known as dimension A) and an extension element (known as dimension B) which can be either drugs or SRE focused. It is a programme jointly funded by the DoH and DfES. The process of certification is based on assessed training needs, supported continuing professional development (CPD) to meet the individual training needs, the collection of evidence within a portfolio to demonstrate the achievement of core and extension standards, initial submission and reflection upon feedback, then final submission. For further information see http://www.wiredforhealth.gov.uk.

Assessing your levels of participation and engagement

Use the following photocopiable resources as tools to help assess and manage your participation and engagement with wider partners. Adding in Arnstein's ladder of participation can help you understand your current levels of engagement and to identify where new partnerships could be made as well as areas for development.

Identifying Your Key Partners

To be completed by the team

Frequency of contact codes: D = daily, W = weekly, M= Monthly, T = Termly, B = Biannual, A = Annual, O = Occasional but not regular

Agency	Name	Contact telephone	Contact address	Contact e-mail	Frequency of contact

Paul Chapman Publishing 2007 © Emma Croghan

Key Contact Diary

To be completed by all members of the team

Photocopy this page and keep in a file. Whenever you have a health promotion contact with another agency partner complete and file. This way you will be able to identify your key change agents who support your health promotion aims and objectives.

Date	Contact Name	Contact cause	What happened? (reflection)	Next action (planning and reflection)

Paul Chapman Publishing 2007 © Emma Croghan

Self-assessment of current partnership work for health promotion

To be completed by school lead

What contact do you currently have with the following agencies?

Partner	Never	Occasional/ ad hoc	Quarterly	Monthly	Weekly
Education					
School health					
Social services					
Transport					
Environment					
Council					
Acute health					
Community health					
Voluntary groups (please name)					
Private sector (please name)					
Other: please state					

CHAPTER 6

Foundation Stage and health promotion

Chapter aims

Primary socialisation theories and theories of child development both suggest that if health promotion activities start and are contextualised at an early age, children are more likely to adopt these behaviours for life. This chapter examines what could be happening to promote the health of Foundation Stage pupils. Engaging children and having an atmosphere which aims for positive outcomes and reaching individual health potential rather than fear of negative consequences of ill health behaviours is essential with very small children who have limited control over their diet and other lifestyle behaviours. These behaviours, over which they may exert little control, may affect their physical, social or emotional health and well-being now and in the future.

Promoting physical health

As discussed earlier, one of the main risks to children of this age in terms of their physical health and well-being, which also impacts upon both social and emotional well-being, is the risk of respiratory and gastro-intestinal infections. At an early stage on entry to school, it is important to teach children about the importance of hygiene in reducing the risks of cross con-tamination. The Department for Education and Skills state that at Foundation/Key Stage 1 all pupils 'should be taught to maintain personal hygiene... [and] ... how some diseases can be spread and controlled' (see DfES National Curriculum for PSHE website).

Lesson plan 6.1 describing a lesson about hand washing and nose blowing has been used with children in pre-school and Reception classes. The comparable rates of sickness absence in the groups who had participated in the lesson reduced by 9 per cent (14 per cent at baseline (winter) to 5 per cent at follow-up (winter)). A questionnaire was sent to parents prior to the lesson (baseline) and the term following the lesson (follow-up), which showed increases in 'appropriate' hand washing activity (i.e. after touching an animal, after visiting the toilet, before meals), and decreases in children needing a prompt from parents or carers prior to washing their hands. Parents/carers were also asked to describe how their children behaved when they had a runny nose. Most children prior to the lesson used material handkerchiefs (48 per cent) and/or reused paper tissues (62 per cent). Following the lesson, and for at least a year afterwards, children were eight times more likely to use a paper tissue once and then dispose of it, than to use any other mechanism (Croghan, 2004).

This clearly demonstrated that a short lesson with some homework to do with parents aimed at children at the very beginning of their school career may be effective at reducing sickness absence, and also teaches children the appropriate mechanisms for control of infections.

Foundation Stage Physical Health

Teacher notes

Aims: For children to understand the importance of appropriate hand washing and nose blowing to prevent the spread of infections

Objectives: For children to engage with 'Bully Bug'

For children to identify hand washing as a key activity to help with health

For children to identify nose blowing as a key activity for health

For children to practise hand washing

For children to associate paper tissues with healthful activity

For parents to reinforce activities with home work

Suggested outcomes:

Visual survey pre and post of natural behaviours of children or a small-scale survey

Groupings: Small groups of up to 6 with similar strengths

Partners: Parents/carers invited to participate and informed about planned lesson

School health nurses invited to participate

School cook/lunchtime supervisors invited to participate

Time for lesson:

20–30 minutes, split into smaller (maximum 10-minute) activities

Teaching styles included – Visual (V), Auditory (A) and Kinaesthetic (K)

Resources: 'Bully Bug' story

Paper tissues (1 box per table) and material handkerchief

Liquid soap and warm water (1 per table)

Towels (1 per table)

Cut-out pictures (resource 1) and Blu-tack

Paper and coloured crayons/pencils

Washable pen (1 per table)

Activity	Time	Rationale	Resource required
Discussion in the round (VA) Ask children what it means to be 'healthy' What can they do to help themselves be healthy? What do you do if you have a cold? Does it make your nose wet or dry? *Demonstration (helper/ parents and other adults present)* 'Sneeze' into handkerchief (add water) Response: 'Bless you!'	5 mins	For children to consider the concept of healthy as more than 'not being unwell' Cloth handkerchief	
Art: with one adult per table (VA) Children work at putting things which help us to be healthy into 'Help Us to Be Healthy' book (Resource 6.1) Invite children in pairs to come and choose an item which helps us to be healthy and say why Discuss each following item: Bath: helps us to get clean and wash any dirt and germs away	10 mins	To allow children to touch and participate in identifying the things which help promote health	Blu-tack, board, cut outs (resource 1)

Activity	Time	Rationale	Resource required
Toothbrush: helps keep our teeth clean so we can chew our food Soap: helps to grab hold of the bugs and dirt so that they come off our body and hands Box of tissues: helps us to catch the bugs and throw them away			
Hand washing (VK) Children go to their tables in small groups with one adult per table Draw a bug on adult hand Take the wet handkerchief from colleague ('Ugh! It's all wet!') 'Bully Bug' is now on your hand: from the wet handkerchief! What do the children think he is trying to do? Show them how you can wash him off using soap and warm water Ask helpers to draw 'Bully' on each child's hand Help children to wash him off: who washed him off first?	10 mins	To allow children to visualise 'germs' and 'bugs' and to visualise the importance of hand washing to remove them	Wet handkerchief Soap and water Towel

Activity	Time	Rationale	Resource required
Nose blowing in the round 'Now 'Bully Bug' is gone, what shall we do with his brothers and sisters who have come from [helper] and want to give me their cold?' Helper starts to sneeze Offer helper paper tissue Helper sneezes into paper tissue 'We can put them in the bin: and they can keep their cold to themselves!' Scrumple tissues and put in the bin		For children to problem-solve the idea	
Poem and song together (VA) Read 'Bully Bug' poem Finish with 'Here We Go Round The Healthy Tree': all children standing in a circle with helpers		To reinforce the messages from the whole lesson	
Take home Activity Sheets 1 and 2 (Resources 6.4 and 6.5)		To reinforce the messages from the whole lesson and involve parents/carers	

What helps us to stay healthy pictures:

Here we go round the healthy tree, the healthy tree, the healthy tree

Here we go round the healthy tree, the healthy tree, the healthy tree

Here we go round the healthy tree on a cold and frosty morning.

This is the way we wash our hands, wash our hands, wash our hands

This is the way we wash our hands, wash our hands, wash our hands

This is the way we wash our hands to keep ourselves clean
and healthy.

This is the way we blow our nose, blow our nose, blow our nose

This is the way we blow our nose, blow our nose, blow our nose

This is the way we blow our nose, to keep ourselves nice and healthy.

Bully Bugs are all around

They try to make us ill

They're bugs and they don't make a sound

Water and tissues are their pill

They want to get inside your tum

So they can make you poorly-oh

After the toilet when your done

Wash hands to make bugs go-go-go

Wash your hands quick quick quick

Before you eat your food

Bully Bugs make you sick sick sick

And that is really rude

They like to give you coughs and sneezes

And jump from throat to nose

So blow your noses, 1,2,3 sneeze

And into the bin bug goes.

To the tune of: 'Twinkle Twinkle, Little Star'

Twinkle, twinkle runny nose

Let's make sure Bully Bug goes

Blow him into a big soft tissue

Wrap him, bin him, clever old you

Now Bully Bug is in the bin

Know this rhyme and you will win

Name: _____

What things help to keep us clean and healthy?
Can you draw a line from the body part to the helper.

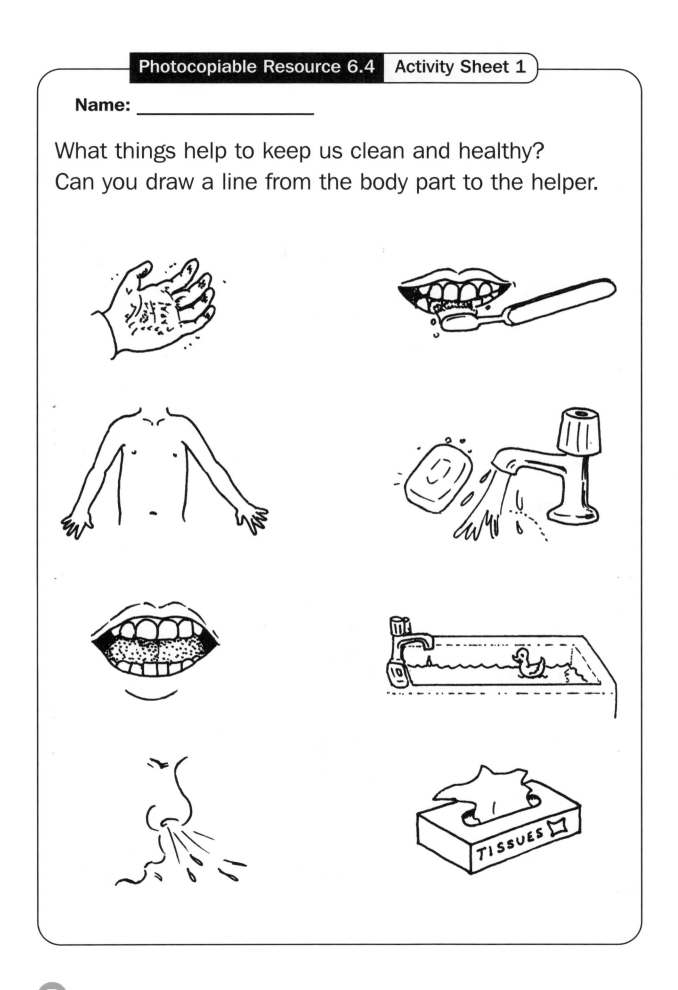

Name: _____

When should we wash our hands? Put a circle around the times you think we need to wash our hands

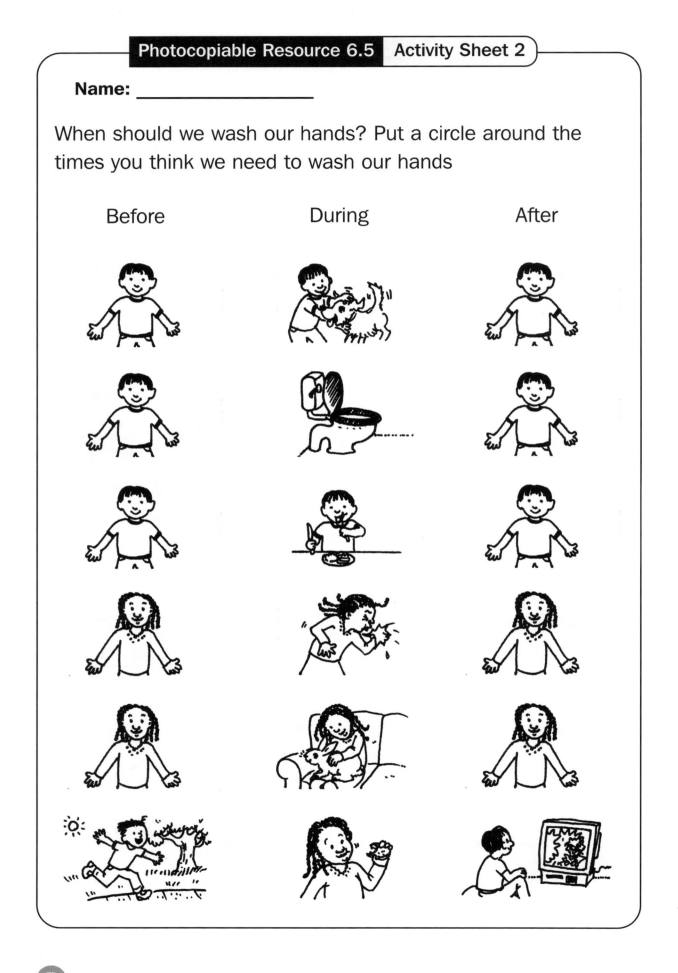

Before · During · After

Promoting emotional health

As discussed in Chapter 3 on the promotion of emotional health and well-being, starting school can be an anxious time for young children, especially for those who have little experience of parental or carer separation. The lesson plan included here has been used with preschool and reception children to help them to feel secure and settled, and to help them feel a sense of comfort and familiarity in a new situation. It can be used in conjunction with other activities, such as staggered introduction to school, to help children feel emotionally secure.

Foundation Stage Emotional Health

Teacher notes

Aims: For children to feel secure about themselves and develop a sense of self-comfort and resilience

Objectives: To promote development emotionally, creatively, intellectually and spiritually

To initiate and develop mutually satisfying personal relationships

To allow the pupils to safely face problems, resolve them and learn from them

To develop confidence and assertiveness skills

To begin to become aware of others and empathise with them

To play and have fun

To laugh

To provide a permanent tool for the use of pupils to support their emotional comfort at times of stress

Suggested outcomes:

Completion of Activity Sheet 3 and the continued reinforcement of the Happy Book

Groupings: Circle time, then small groups (maximum 6) per table

Partners: Parents/carers invited to participate and informed about planned lesson. One parent per table to support the art and consideration of themes

Time for lesson:

30 minutes (in small sessions of 10 minutes) + 10 minutes' art + next day follow-up

Resources: The 'Ugly Duckling' story book

A cuddly duck

Sheet of paper per child

Coloured pencils and crayons

Teaching styles included – Visual (V), Auditory (A) and Kinaesthetic (K)

Take home activities:

Happy Book parent/helper sheet (Resource 6.7)

Activity	Time	Rationale	Resource required
Sitting in a circle introduce the concept of circle time (VAK). Introduce the duck 'Happy'. Whoever holds the duck can speak and everyone else has to listen to them. Happy will come to everyone, so everyone can say something. Pass Happy round: What or who makes you feel happy?	10 mins	To promote development emotionally, creatively, intellectually and spiritually To develop confidence and assertiveness skills To initiate and develop mutually satisfying personal relationships	Cuddly duck
Read 'The Ugly Duckling' to the saddest part when the duckling is laughed at and feels sad.	5 mins	To begin to become aware of others and empathise with them	The ugly duckling
How do you think the duck feels? Why? Pass 'Happy' to pupils with hands up prior to response. Continue reading to the end of the story. How do you think the swan feels? Why? (AK) Pass 'Happy' to pupils with hands up prior to response.	5 mins	To begin to become aware of others and empathise with them To begin to become aware of others and empathise with them	Cuddly duck The ugly duckling Cuddly duck

▶

Activity	Time	Rationale	Resource required
Pass 'Happy' round to all children. How did that story make you feel?	10 mins	To begin to become aware of others and empathise with them	Cuddly duck
Children to tables (VA). Parent/helper: Close your eyes and think of something that makes you feel happy when you see it, touch it, smell it, hear it. What do you think of? Draw a picture of your happy thought. Make it very colourful and we will put all of your happy thoughts into a book.	10 mins	To promote development emotionally, creatively, intellectually and spiritually	Paper and pencils/crayons
Collate pictures into a book. Cover with a front cover (Resource 6.6). Show children the book (VA). Go through each picture. Put in the classroom: children can touch, look at and feel the book (K) whenever they feel a bit sad and they need a happy thought.	After the lesson The next day	To allow the pupils to safely face problems, resolve them and learn from them	Resource 6.6

Our Happy Book

Class

We made this book to help us feel happy when we feel sad, worried or scared

Our Happy Book

What makes you feel happy? Can you draw a picture of the things that make you happy?

Make it colourful and we will be able to put it together into our class book.

Name: _____

How do these people feel? With your parent or helper, draw a line from the right word to the right face.

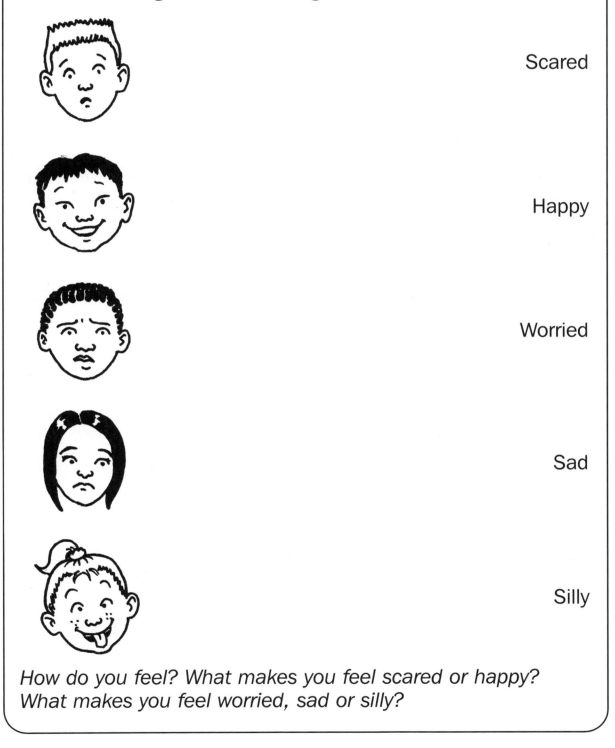

Scared

Happy

Worried

Sad

Silly

How do you feel? What makes you feel scared or happy?
What makes you feel worried, sad or silly?

Promoting social health

As discussed in Chapter 4 on the promotion of social health in the whole school and also as referred to in the previous chapter, children beginning school need to feel part of the school community. This will lessen their feelings of insecurity in the grown-up world of school associated with isolation from their normal environment and promote emotional health in the Early Years setting. The four key concepts which will enable children to feel a sense of community belonging and engender social health through partnership are:

- feeling a sense of membership or belonging;
- having a sense of influence/ability to effect change;
- developing shared values;
- developing shared emotional connections.

Lesson Plan 6.3 described below has been used with Reception children to help them identify mechanisms through which they can influence change.

Foundation Stage Social Health (1)

Teacher notes

Aims: For children to feel a sense of community

Objectives: For pupils to feel a sense of membership or belonging
For pupils to have a sense of influence/ability to effect change
For pupils to develop shared values
For pupils to develop shared emotional connections

Suggested outcomes:
A collation of pictures about the class rules by the children

Groupings: Small groups of up to 6, with one adult (parent/helper) per group

Partners: Parents/carers invited to participate and informed about
planned lesson
Local MP or councillor invited

Time for lesson:
30–45 minutes, split into 10-minute activities

Resources: School song (if there is one)
School motto (if there is one)
Paper
Paints
Collage materials
Teaching styles included – Visual (V), Auditory (A) and
Kinaesthetic (K)

Take home activities:
Activity Sheet 4 (Resource 6.9)

Activity	Time	Rationale	Resource required
Teach children the school song/motto if there is one. (A) What are the school rules? (VA)	5–10 mins	For pupils to feel a sense of membership or belonging For pupils to develop shared values For pupils to develop shared emotional connections	School song/motto/rules
What should our class rules be? Write down on the board everything which is suggested as a rule. How do we know which ones to choose if we can only choose 4 or 5? Ask for ideas? Suggest voting: what does voting mean? Should the teacher choose or should everyone get a chance to choose? (VA)	10 mins	For pupils to have a sense of influence/ability to effect change	Board and pens
Vote for each item suggested, using a consensus line. (AK)	5 mins	For pupils to have a sense of influence/ability to effect change	Board and pens
Agree through consensus the top 3 or 4 things.	5 mins	For pupils to develop shared values	Board and pens

Activity	Time	Rationale	Resource required
Can everyone try and keep to these rules? What might stop us? What should we do if we break the rules?	5 mins	For pupils to develop shared values For pupils to develop shared values	Board and pens
Group art Make a collage or paint the class rules together, moving around as it is done. (K) Display on a classroom wall.	Remaining time and follow-up	To reinforce the values and work that has been undertaken	Art materials

Rules: Family Work

Name of child:

Does your family have rules?

Talk together with your child about the family rules.

Our family rules are:

1 _____
2 _____
3 _____
4 _____
5 _____

What rule would your child like to put into the family rules?

1 _____
2 _____
3 _____
4 _____
5 _____

Ask your child to tell you the rules to their favourite game.

Favourite game:

The rules:

Ask them to draw a picture of playing the game on the back of this sheet.

Foundation Stage Social Health (2)

Teacher notes

Aims: For children to feel a sense of community

Objectives: For pupils to feel a sense of membership or belonging

For pupils to have a sense of influence/ability to effect change

For pupils to develop shared values

For pupils to develop shared emotional connections

Suggested outcome:

A corporate class badge or logo which has been agreed

Partners: Parents/carers invited to participate and informed about planned lesson

Local MP or councillor invited

Time for lesson:

30–45 minutes, split into 5- or 10-minute activities

Resources: School uniform

White cardboard discs (for badges)

Coloured pencils

Teaching styles included – Visual (V), Auditory (A) and Kinaesthetic (K)

Groupings: Mainly small groups of up to 6, with one adult helper or parent per group

Take home activities:

Take home badge and talk about it with parents/carers

Activity	Time	Rationale	Resource required
Discussion (A) What is the school uniform? Why do we wear the uniform? How do we know who is in which house/team in school?	5 mins	For pupils to feel a sense of membership or belonging For pupils to develop shared values For pupils to develop shared emotional connections	
Art (VA) What would you like the uniform to look like? On your picture, colour in the uniform that you would choose.	10 mins	For pupils to have a sense of influence/ability to effect change	
Discussion (A) How can we tell who is in our class? Can we decide on a class badge so that everyone knows what class we are in? What colour should it be? Should it have a picture on it?	5 mins	For pupils to develop shared values	
Voting – stand on a consensus line (AK)	5 mins	For pupils to develop shared values	

Activity	Time	Rationale	Resource required
Art Colour badges as per group design. (V) Everyone wears badge for the next week.	5–10 mins	For pupils to develop shared values To reinforce messages	

CHAPTER 7

Reception to Year 3 and health promotion

Chapter aims

This chapter refers to the most important health risks in this age group and provides lesson plans as examples of how professionals can work to empower students to avoid risk.

It considers how to evaluate the health of children in their particular school area in terms of the risk of the locality and looks at what special activities could be undertaken to promote the health of Key Stage 1 pupils. This chapter also focuses on examples of good practice which have achieved positive outcomes.

Promoting physical health in Key Stage 1

This is the period during which children are becoming more independent physically in and around the home. Children usually begin to pedal bicycles or tricycles at 2 years of age and are expert peddlers by 4 years. Many children begin to ride a bicycle without stabilisers from 5–6 years of age. They are also becoming more confident and independent in and around water and in and around the home. Avoiding accidents and learning to identify and avoid physical risk is an important goal for this group. Inviting key partners like RoSPA, the local police or fire-lighters in to talk about these issues will engage children and help them to identify risk and strategies for avoiding risk.

It is also the age at which lifestyle education, including obesity and smoking prevention, become key strategies in developing healthy lifestyles.

Promoting Physical Health at KS1 (1)

Teacher notes

Aims: For children to understand the importance of physical activity as a health enhancer

Objectives: For pupils to have an understanding of the physiological effects of exercise

For pupils to witness the physiological consequences of activity in context

For energy output to be considered in the context of a balance to be achieved

Partners: Physical activity lead from local health organisation (if available)

School health nurse

Time for lesson: 45 minutes, split into 10-minute activities

Suggested outcomes:

Display of the before and after pyramids, showing some change in applications

Resources: Exercise pyramid handouts (Resource 7.1)

Stopwatch

Teaching styles included – Visual (V), Auditory (A) and Kinaesthetic (K)

Take home activities:

Local activities information, leaflet (Such as the *Let's Get Physical Pocket Play Pack* to show children that physical activity is all part of their everyday play – and is fun. This pack is filled with ideas that show what fun it can be to be physically active. It includes charts for children to record and gradually increase the amount of time they spend being active (available from British Heart Foundation 2005, http://www.bhf.org.uk).

Activity	Time	Rationale	Resource required
Discussion – in the round What is physical activity? Show one child sitting, one walking one running on the spot. (VK) Why do we do it? Introduce the concept of the activity pyramid and talk it through with the children. (VA)	5 mins	To introduce the concept of healthful physical activity	Board and pens
Art – small groups at tables What is their current activity level? Draw on the pyramid the activity you do.	10 mins	To assess baseline activity levels	Pyramids, pencils/crayons
Science – in the round Choose three children. What do the children know about healthy hearts? Does being active make your heart work more, less, or no differently? Take the children's pulses over one minute and record.	5 mins	To allow children to question and problem-solve	
Split the children into three groups. Identify each group with one of the children you have chosen. One of the three identified children sits on a chair, one slowly walks up and down, one jumps up and down on the spot for one minute.	1 min	To allow visualisation	Stopwatch
Take the three children's pulses and record. (VAK)	1 min		Stopwatch
Ask the groups to guess what has happened to the pulse of each child (up, down or stayed the same)? Show the results. Was it as expected?	5 mins	To allow children to problem-solve	Board and pens
Ask the children to complete a second pyramid (aspirational) to decide what they would like to change of anything to increase their level of physical activity.	10 mins	To allow children to question and problem-solve	Pyramids, pencils/crayons
Take home leaflet (available from British Heart Foundation, local health care providers, etc.).		To reinforce messages and to gain parental support	

Extra optional activity – 10-mins activity outside (K). How do they feel before and afterwards?

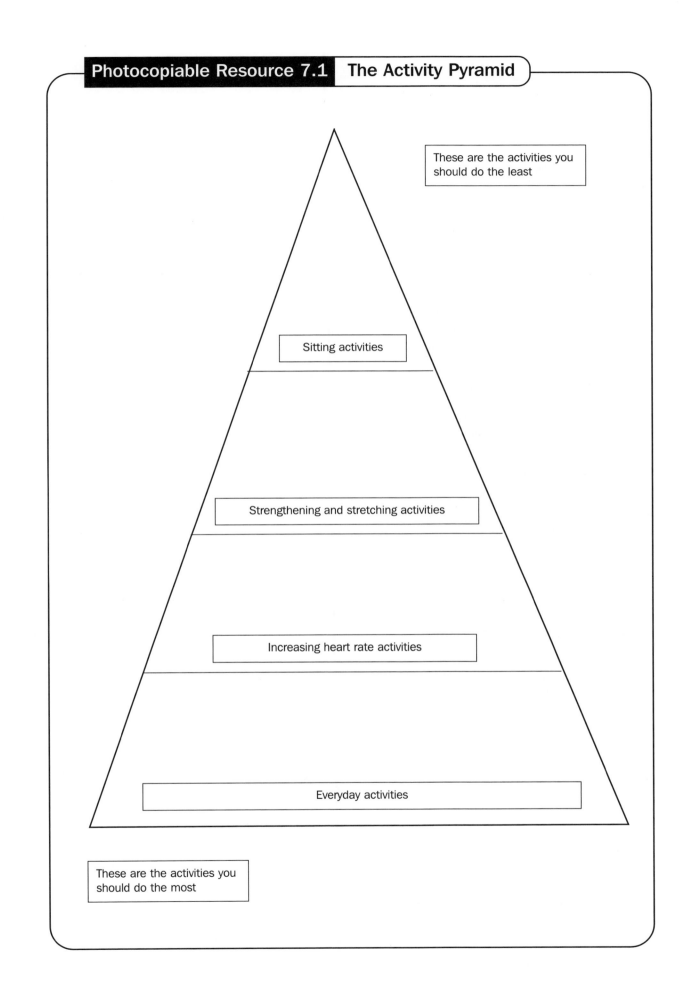

These are the activities you should do the least

Sitting activities

Strengthening and stretching activities

Increasing heart rate activities

Everyday activities

These are the activities you should do the most

Promoting Physical Health at KS1 (2)

Teacher notes

Aims:	For children to understand the importance of a balanced diet in supporting health
Objectives:	For pupils to have an understanding of the importance of good nutrition For children to feel that food is fun For children to have an understanding of the concepts of the balance of good health and how this can be applied to them.

Suggested outcomes:

Change in demonstrated balance of good health food (BGH) plates

Partners: School health nurse
School cook

Time for lesson:

45 minutes, split into shorter 10-minute max. actiivites

Resources: Balance of good health

Pictures of food from magazines

Large copies of balance of good health empty plate (resource 10): 1 per table

Teaching styles included – Visual (V), Auditory (A) and Kinaesthetic (K)

Take home activities:

Resource 7.2: Planning a healthy hearts party
Healthy recipe ideas in school newsletter

Activity	Time	Rationale required	Resource
Discussion/brainstorm in the round Who likes eating: what is your favourite food? Food should be fun! Show different foods. (VA) What is a 'healthy diet'? What foods are healthy/unhealthy? Do you always eat 'healthy' food?	5 mins	For children to identify their perceptions	Board and pens
Introduce the concept of 'the balance of good health' (BGH) BGH is based on five food groups. Choosing a variety of foods from the first four groups every day will provide the body with the wide range of nutrients which it needs. Foods in the fifth group – foods containing fat and foods containing sugar – are not essential to a healthy diet but add extra variety, choice and palatability to meals. This group of foods should form the smallest part of the diet. Talk briefly about the different food types. Show one or two items from each food group – tasting if possible (VAK): Protein: for strength and growth. Carbohydrate: for healthy growth. Fruits and vegetables: give us vitamins and minerals. Dairy: good source of calcium, good for healthy teeth and bones. Fats and sugary food: taste nice but no nutritional benefit.	5 mins	To provide information	Board and pens, BGH leaflets
Put the children into five small groups, each named after a food group. Ask each group to find pictures of one of the types of food groups (e.g. Proteins find protein-rich food). Ask them to stick their food pictures onto the large BGH plate (VAK).	10 mins	To visualise the concept	Magazines, scissors, glue, large BGH plate
Using a blank template can the children write or draw the foods they like which fit onto their plate (VK)?	10 mins	To visualise the concept	Blank BGH plate
Take home leaflet (available from local healthcare provider).		To reinforce messages	

Planning a healthy hearts party

What healthy fun food will you have at your party? Draw or write here:

What healthy activities will you do at your party? Draw or write here:

Draw/write your invitations here:

Promoting Physical Health at KS1 (3)

Teacher notes

Aims: For children to understand the importance of both a balanced diet and the use of physical activity in supporting health

Objectives: For pupils to have their knowledge of nutrition reinforced
For children to feel that food is fun
For children to have an understanding of the energy in–energy out balance

Suggested outcomes:
Children to be able to identify the different food groups and types within them and to have discussed and understood the concept of energy balance

Partners: School health nurse
School cook

Time for lesson:
45 minutes, split into shorter 10-minute segments of activity

Resources: Balance of good health
Stopwatch
Scales and weights (if possible)
Pencils or crayons
Cut-out pictures (Resource 7.4)
Scales (Resource 7.5)
Teaching styles included – Visual (V), Auditory (A) and Kinaesthetic (K)

Take home activities:
The lunchtime challenge
Colourful food game (Resource 7.6)

Activity	Time	Rationale	Resource required
Small groups of up to 6 Ask children to look at their BGH plates and their activity pyramids. *Class question* How does food and activity balance? Introduce the idea of energy in as calories.	5 mins	For children to have the concept of balancing energy in and energy out	BGH and pyramid (completed)
Take an item of food: show a picture or a packet or an item, including a chocolate bar, a banana, and some cereal. Each equals a weight on the scales. Some foods have more 'weight' on the scales or calories than others (VAK). How can we balance the scales?	5 mins	Energy in concepts	Pictures: Resource 7.4 Scales and weights
Show pictures of sunbather, footballer and swimmer (Resource 7.4) – ask three children to be these people (VAK). How much energy does each of these need? Who has the most? Who will need least energy in? Equally, we all need some energy in, even if we are doing very little, because our bodies are working. Drinks: water gives no weight to energy in, but helps with energy available to use: what about others? Is milk a food or a drink? Drinking some water – how does it taste? How does it feel? (VAK)?	10 mins	Energy out and balancing concepts	Pictures: Resource 7.4 Scales and weights
Using the scales (Resource 7.5), how can the children balance what they have eaten with their activity? *The lunchtime challenge* Can you choose a healthy option (K)?	10 mins	Energy out and balancing concepts	Resource 7.5 Coloured pencils, crayons

The Family Rainbow Challenge Tally Chart

How many naturally coloured foods do you eat? Over a week, see who in your family can eat the most naturally coloured fruit or vegetables. Add up the scores at the end of the week to see who is the rainbow challenge champion!

Name of family member (e.g. Mum, Dad, Bob)	Example Bob					
Beige = 0 points (e.g. chips)	0 + 0 + 0 + 0 = 0					
Green = 1 point per portion (e.g. beans, peas, broccoli)	1 + 1 + 1 + 1 = 4					
Yellow = 2 points per portion (e.g. sweetcorn, bananas, yellow plums)	2 + 2 = 4					
Red = 3 points per portion (e.g. tomatoes, strawberries, sweet potatoes)	3 + 3 + 3 + 3 = 12					
Orange = 4 points per portion (e.g. orange, swede, pumpkin)	4 + 4 = 8					
Purple = 5 points per portion (e.g. aubergine, beetroot, plums)	5 + 5 = 10					
Totals	38					

Promoting emotional health in Key Stage 1

It has been suggested that a healthy school actively seeks to promote positive emotional health and well-being and helps pupils to understand and express their feelings and build their confidence and emotional resilience to learn.

Following the adjustment by pupils from the home-centred preschool environment, the years from Reception or school entry through to Year 3 and the end of infant school offer children many new experiences and new opportunities. For some children, these opportunities increase anxiety, while others are able independently to deal with issues. Promoting emotional health in this age group essentially means allowing open and honest discussions and facilitation of conflict management where necessary. A key element is also that children should be playing and having fun, laughing and enjoying life and school as part of their life. The Happy Book used by children in Early Years can be adapted so that older children can use the concept.

Other ideas, such as guided relaxation (see below), can be used with some groups. Guided relaxation techniques are best introduced to children at the end of physical activity interventions such as PE. They can lie down at the end of the session and can be guided to take 'belly breaths' with a hand on their tummies to ensure that they are breathing to full lung capacity. At the same time, they can be guided through a process of relaxation, where they are encouraged to clench muscle groups and relax them in turn, starting from the toes.

Guided relaxation: example

Lying down, make sure you are comfortable. Put one hand on your tummy and the other at your side. When you take a deep breath in through your nose, your tummy rises up and gets bigger. When you breathe out, your tummy should go down. Take a deep breath in now, hold it 2, 3, 4 and let it out through your mouth as if you are blowing up a balloon.

Deep breath in, 2, 3, 4, and out 2, 3, 4.

Deep breath in, 2, 3, 4 and out 2, 3, 4.

Keep breathing in and out slowly … with your next breath in, imagine pulling your toes up towards the sky, and with your breath out … let them go. Next straighten your legs so that they are stiff, and with your breath out let them relax. Next clench your bottom together with your breath in (usually much laughter at this point!) and let it relax with your breath out … now suck your tummy in and then let it out, now shrug your shoulders, and relax them with your breath out. Next screw your hands up really tightly, and with your breath out let them relax. With your next breath in screw up your faces – I want to see some really scary faces! – and when you breathe out relax your face.

Now breathe in, 2, 3, 4 and out, 2, 3, 4, in, 2, 3, 4 and out 2, 3, 4.

Start to have a little wriggle and open your eyes.

Slowly sit forward and stretch your arms up to the sky. Wiggle them down to the floor again and we're done!

Promoting Emotional Health at KS1

Teacher notes

Aims: For children to feel secure about themselves as individuals

Objectives: To promote development emotionally, creatively, intellectually and spiritually
To initiate and develop mutually satisfying personal relationships
To allow the pupils to face problems safely, resolve them and learn from them
To develop confidence and assertiveness skills
To begin to become aware of others and empathise with them
To play and have fun
To laugh

Partners: Parents/carers invited to participate and are informed about planned lesson – ask each helper or parent to sit at a table so that there is one adult per table

Time for lesson: 30–45 minutes, split into smaller 10-minute maximum activities

Suggested outcome:
Each table to have discussed similarity and difference

Resources: Resource 7.7: What Makes Me Special?
Resource 7.8: My Friends and Me
Resource 7.9: Guess the Photo
Teaching styles included – Visual (V), Auditory (A) and Kinaesthetic (K)

Paul Chapman Publishing 2007 © Emma Croghan

Activity	Time	Rationale	Resource required
Invite children to bring in a photo of themselves as a baby. Put all the pictures onto a backing board.	Pre-lesson		Photos of children Backing board
Children complete Resource 7.7: What Makes Me Special? (VA).	10 mins	To allow them to identify positive aspects of themselves	Resource 7.7
Children complete in groups Resource 7.8: My Friends and Me (VAK).	10 mins	To allow them to identify positive aspects of each other	Resource 7.8
Guess the child in Resource 7.9 (VAK).	10 mins	To allow them to laugh with each other and discover something unusual	Resource 7.9
Feedback: what were the correct answers?	5–10 mins		

What Makes Me Special?

This is all about you. Imagine you are telling someone new all about yourself.

What is your name?

How old are you?

When is your birthday?

Where do you live?

Do you have any brothers or sisters and what are their names?

What is special about you?

Can you see it, or is it something inside you, like kindness?

Draw a picture of you: can you see what is special? How could you show it?

My Friends and Me

Working at your tables, talk to your friends.

Draw your table. Can you show where each person sits?

Does everyone have the same colour hair?

How many have brown hair?

How many have black hair?

How many have red hair?

How many have blonde hair?

Does everyone have the same colour eyes?

How many have blue eyes?

How many have green eyes?

How many have brown eyes?

Is everyone the same?

Working with the person sitting next to you:

What makes them different?

What makes them special?

What do you like most about them?

What do they like most about you?

How does it make you feel talking to them?

(smiley face)   (straight face)   (sad face)

Guess the Photo

Who do you think each photograph is? (Don't forget the teachers!)

Move around the room to look at the photos.

Write the name of the person you think is shown in each baby photograph:

1 _____
2 _____
3 _____
4 _____
5 _____
6 _____
7 _____
8 _____
9 _____
10 _____
11 _____
12 _____
13 _____
14 _____
15 _____
16 _____
17 _____
18 _____
19 _____
20 _____
21 _____
22 _____
23 _____
24 _____
25 _____
26 _____
27 _____
28 _____
29 _____
30 _____

Promoting social health in Key Stage 1

During the Key Stage 1 period, children may be joining clubs such as dancing, Rainbows/Brownies, Beavers/Cubs, etc., all of which will enhance their sense of belonging to a wider community. Some children will not be accessing these; however, whether they do or not, school remains for most children the central and defining element of their experience of community.

An important early teaching aim is the understanding that everyone is different and everyone has a contribution to make. Lesson Plan 7.5 described below has been used with children in both Year 1 and Year 2 to support this.

Promoting Social Health and Well-being at KS1

Teaching notes

Aims:	To encourage community awareness
Objectives:	For all pupils to feel a sense of membership/belonging For all children to feel they have influence/ability to effect change For children to develop shared values For children to develop shared emotional connections
Time for lesson:	30 minutes + 30 minutes (split into shorter segments)

🏁 Suggested outcomes:

A consensus and a change in a physical element of the classroom

📋 Resources: Resource 7.10
Resource 7.11
Learning styles included – Visual (V), Auditory (A) and Kinaesthetic (K)

Activity	Time	Rationale	Resource required
Ask the class to work in small groups (max. 6). Each group should identify the one thing it would like to change about the classroom. They may move around the classroom to examine things (VAK). Why change it?	10 mins	For all pupils to feel a sense of membership/belonging For children to develop shared emotional connections	Resource 7.10
Each group should prepare an argument for why their change should happen, with pictures of how the room would look and how this would improve class life for everyone (VA).	10 mins	For all children to feel they have to influence/ability effect change	
Each group should present their argument: with up to three reasons why the change should happen (VA). Put the pictures up in the classroom for one week (VK).	10 mins	For children to develop shared values	
At the end of one week ask the children to complete Resource 7.11 in small groups.	15 mins	For children to develop shared values	Resource 7.11
Community vote and discussion: which idea should be taken; if agreement is not reached, no change happens.	15 mins	For all children to feel they have influence/ability to effect change	
Use a consensus line for voting – stand on an imaginary line, or in a certain physical space (e.g. corners of the room) to show which you agree with (AK).	15 mins		

One sheet per group.

In your groups, think about what you would like to change in your classroom.

Can you decide on one thing to change in your group? Have you looked closely, or touched the area you would like to change?

Why would you like it to change?

If your change happens, who will it be better for?

Why?

How will things be better for everyone?

Why?

Why hasn't it already changed?

Do you think everyone else will agree with your group?

Why?

Look at each idea for changing your classroom. Walk around and look at what they would like to change.

Which do you like best?

Why?

If the change you like best happened who would it help?

Who would it not help?

Which does your group like best?

Why?

If the change your group likes best happened who would it help?

Who would it not help?

Which will you vote for?

CHAPTER 8

Key Stage 2 and health promotion

Chapter aims

This chapter aims to consider the special requirements of health promotion for this age group and to provide opportunities and ideas for supporting and encouraging health promotion activities for them.

Puberty

Puberty may begin in some girls at around age 7–8, and for some boys at around age 9–10. Physical and emotional changes around these times may be confusing for children, especially if they are early developers and feel isolated by their body changes. It is important that these issues are raised early in the 'junior' school career of the child. It is also important that parents are informed and offered the opportunity to talk to their children prior to any school information. Much of the physical, emotional and social health promotion for this age group needs to be sensitively delivered around the sex and relationships education (SRE) agenda.

The DfES states that parents should be consulted by their child's school about its SRE policy and informed about what is taught in the SRE lesson. Parents/carers have the right to withdraw their child from some, or all, SRE lessons, but not statutory science lessons (DfES, 2005c).

Promoting physical and emotional health at Key Stage 2

Rather than individual lesson plans to be used in isolation, a plan for the natural integration of SRE into other curriculum areas should be developed. This should promote SRE as part of the wider physical and emotional literacy agenda, so that SRE is part of the continuum of lifelong health promotion.

The main questions to be answered at this time period are:

Physical

- What changes happen to make girls women and boys men?
- Where do babies come from?
- Awareness of good touching and bad touching.

Emotional

- Can boys and girls be friends?
- How do we say no to someone without upsetting them?

Social

- What are some of the main differences between us (males/females)?
- What is the difference between males and females?

There are several partners who can be involved in this strategic visioning and delivery, including school health nurses, healthy schools nurses, voluntary organisations and other local organisations.

Other elements of health promotion which may be considered for this age group are sun safety and sun awareness, and smoking prevention.

Promoting Physical Health at KS 2

Teacher notes

Aims: To improve knowledge, attitudes and behaviour towards not smoking

Objectives: For pupils to have a knowledge of how to resist pressure to smoke
For pupils to broaden their knowledge about smoking
For pupils to become aware of subversive marketing

Suggested outcomes:
Change on the consensus line of 'Is smoking cool?'

Time for lesson: 45 minutes

Resources: What's in a cigarette (available from local health promotion/health organisation)
Art materials
Learning styles included – Visual (V), Auditory and Kinaesthetic (K)

Activity	Time required	Rationale	Resource
Group discussion/brainstorm Why do people smoke (VA)? *Stress*: Cigarettes do not decrease stress; they physiologically increase stress by raising blood pressure and pulse, but smokers feel relaxed because they take lots of deep breaths, they have a break and they like cigarettes. *Addiction*: Nicotine is a very addictive drug – as addictive as other drugs of dependence – and children very quickly get addicted. The people who make cigarettes earn lots of money and want more people to smoke so they can keep getting more money. They think it's cool – is it cool? Stand on a consensus line – cool to not cool. Can you say why you think that? (AK) No, it is an addiction, smokers smell, their teeth are not so nice as non-smokers' and it costs lots of money.	10 mins	To allow pupils to establish fact *vs* fiction	Board and pens
What's in a cigarette?	5 mins	To allow pupils to establish fact *vs* ficton	Prop/ leaflet
Why do people want to stop and why do they find it hard? (VA) Addiction Money *Health*: smoking causes lots of diseases which people would not get if they did not smoke. Anyone who wants to get help to stop smoking can contact their local health care provider.	10 mins	To allow pupils to establish fact *vs* fiction	Board and pens
Create a collage or picture to show that smoking is not cool (VA). Display pictures around the wall.	20 mins	To visualise the message	Art materials
Revisit the consensus line – has anyone changed their mind? Why?	Following lesson	To reinforce message	

Optional extra: Face paint a non-smoking sign on children's cheeks, photograph them and send home the picture with details about local adult stop smoking services. This obviously requires parental consent, but it has been used very effectively in some areas.

(Source: Birmingham Face Facts Programme)

Promoting emotional health at Key Stage 2

Primary school children may experience bullying or be worried about the possibility of bullying, particularly as they become more self-aware and more concerned about not fitting in. Most children at some time are concerned that they are different and a great deal of emotional health promotion for children in schools should focus on helping them to relax and realise that everyone is different and that difference is to be celebrated.

Promoting Emotional Health at KS 2

Teacher notes

Aims: For children to feel secure about themselves as individuals

Objectives: To promote development emotionally, creatively, intellectually and spiritually

To initiate and develop mutually satisfying personal relationships

To allow the pupils to face problems safely, resolve them and learn from them

To develop confidence and assertiveness skills

To begin to become aware of others and empathise with them

To play and have fun

To laugh

Parents/carers invited to participate and informed about planned lesson

Suggested outcomes:
Perceptions of feelings and discussion using the last activity.

Time for lesson:
30–45 minutes

Resources: Drama notes (Resource 8.1)

Learning styles included – Visual (V), Auditory (A) and Kinaesthetic (K)

Activity	Time	Rationale required	Resource
Tell the pupils the story of Ameera and her friends (Resource 8.1) (A).	5 mins	To promote development emotionally, creatively, intellectually and spiritually	Resource 8.1
Ask the children to identify their own ending and act it out with the rest of the story (VAK).	20 mins	To initiate and develop mutually satisfying personal relationships To allow the pupils to safely face problems, resolve them and learn from them To develop confidence and assertiveness skills To play and have fun To laugh	
Debrief: how do they feel each participant felt (Resource 8.2) (VAK), using each corner of the room for a different emotion.	20 mins	To begin to become aware of others and empathise with them	Resource 8.1

Drama Notes

Ameera: 9 years old, lives with her parents and her two younger brothers

Sally: 10 years old, Ameera's best friend since preschool, lives with her mum and older sister

Abigail: soon to be 10, has just moved to the area with her parents and older brother, Robert

Robert: aged 13, Abigail's brother and new best friends with Nick

Tom: aged 9, has been friends with Sally and Ameera since preschool

James: 10 years old, Tom's best friend, lives with his parents and older brother, Nick, next door to Abigail

Nick: aged 12, James's older brother

The situation: Abigail's birthday party

Everyone is at the party. Robert has some cigarettes which he tries to persuade people to take outside and try.

Robert really wants everyone to like him as he is new to the area and he wants to impress Nick so he will be friends with him. Will it work?

Ameera and Sally don't want to be friends with anyone else, but Sally and Ameera's mums both want them to be friends with Abigail.

Abigail feels lonely. She wants to go back to her old home. Her brother is embarrassing her.

Promoting Social Health at KS 2

Teacher notes

Aims: To encourage community awareness

Objectives: For all pupils to feel a sense of membership/belonging
For all children to feel they have influence/ability to effect change
For children to develop shared values
For children to develop shared emotional connections

Suggested outcomes:
Family trees completed

Partners: Parents and carers

Time for lesson:
30–45 minutes

Resources: A picture of each child in class
Information about each child's family
Resource 8.2
Camera
Art materials for tree trunk and branches
Learning styles included – Visual (V), Auditory (A) and Kinaesthetic (K)

Activity	Time	Rationale required	Resource
Children have their photographs taken and put on each branch of a large wall-based tree (VK).	5 mins	For all pupils to feel a sense of membership/belonging	Wall-based tree
Individually (or with parents if invited) children create a personal family tree (Resource 8.2). These can be stuck together with the larger tree near the picture of each child (VA).	Remainder of the lesson	For children to develop shared values For children to develop shared emotional connections	Resource 8.2

Family Tree

CHAPTER 9

Outcomes and evaluations

Chapter aims

This chapter focuses on the inherent difficulties in evaluating health promotion activities with young children and also considers the types of outcomes which could be assessed (process, impact, relevancy, etc.). It also covers disseminating good practice through local and wider networks. Evaluation is a key element of health promotion – what went well and why allows for development of themes and responses to contemporary issues which may arise during the process.

Difficulties in evaluating health promotion

The main difficulties with evaluating health promotion activities , especially in children, are that often it is difficult to isolate the intervention you facilitated when the pupil was in Year 5 as the reason little Johnny did not take up smoking when he was 16. Many other factors may have influenced the decision to make or not to make a healthy or unhealthy choice, which are very difficult to isolate and extricate from each other (advertising, peer pressure, social and family norms). However, professionals are increasingly being asked to provide an evidence base for their activities and to prove they are offering added value.

It is essential to identify what you want to achieve from the health promotion activity prior to the activity. It is also important to ensure that your goals are measurable and realistic, with clear time boundaries. Do you want to affect knowledge, attitudes or behaviour? Why? This will help you to choose the best form of evaluation for your work.

Types of evaluation

There are several types of evaluation available for health promotion.

Outcome

This looks at a defined end point and whether it has been achieved; for example: 'The number of children eating the daily offered piece of fruit increased by 25 per cent following the intervention.' Outcome measurements may reflect changes in knowledge, attitudes, behaviour, skills, self-awareness and decision-making processes. The main outcome measure relates strongly to the initial aim of the intervention – how could this aim be measured? The methods for analysing this range from surveys and questionnaires to interviews and observation.

Process

This examines the effect of different methods or other processes to improve the efficacy of your intervention. For example, noticing that when the teachers ate a piece of fruit with the children, numbers eating the fruit increased, but when the fruit was simply offered to the children and the teachers did not take a piece the consumption decreased. The process can be viewed and evaluated from different perspectives, all of which may be relevant – self-evaluation, client evaluation (this could be school, pupil, family or other stakeholder) or peer evaluation. The main methods for analysing this outcome are surveys and questionnaires, using scales such as the Likert scale which takes five end points and asks respondents to rate their opinion:

Did you feel the lesson went well, overall?

1 Strongly disagree

2 Disagree

3 Neither agree nor disagree

4 Agree

5 Strongly agree

Cost-effectiveness

This allows for strategic decisions to be made concerning the choice of one intervention over another. For example, if a teacher spends one extra hour on an intervention and their hourly rate is £20, the intervention cost £20. What is gained for the £20?

Relevancy

Did the intervention interest the people it aimed to interest? A school nurse who puts on a drop-in clinic in a primary school for children, parents and teachers can assess the relevancy of the service to each of those groups by assessing how many people accessed the service and how they found out about it.

This can also be assessed by identifying the number expected and the number who attended and comparing the two.

Disseminating good practice

Lots of people want to make a difference to the lives and health, educational and social outcomes for children and their wider families. If an intervention happens somewhere, and it works and improves those things for people, other professionals will want to know how and why you did what you did. Evidence-based practice can only happen with evidence of good practice. Some of the ways this can be done are as follows:

- write up the intervention in a professional journal;

- submit an abstract and present at a professional conference;

- tell the local news;

- write about it in the newsletter.

Evaluating and reflecting upon your practice

The following pages contain templates for evaluating each activity to inform the overall evaluation process. This should be done as soon as possible following the activity and wherever possible pupils and the wider community should be asked for feedback.

Following these templates there is a further template for reassessing the school situation following a period of implementing changes to health promotion practice to help you identify further areas of work as well as to provide evidence for a Health Promoting School or NHSP award. These evaluations can be complemented through the use of other tools which you may be more familiar with, such as PASS (Pupil Attitude to School and Self) or the Boxall profile.

However, often the most powerful information and evaluation tool is likely to be one which is done prior to and post any interventions, with a comparison between the two. For example, suppose that in the observations of the class prior to the intervention, 25 per cent of children washed their hands without prompting after going to the toilet. Three months post intervention, 80 per cent of children were observed to be washing their hands without prompting after going to the toilet.

Evaluation Template to Follow Each Activity

To be completed by deliverer of activity

Aim (what did you want to achieve?):

Objectives (how did you plan to achieve the aim?):

Outcome measure (how would you know you had achieved your aim?):

Process measure (how would you tell what worked best?):

Methods (what you did):

Outcome:

Process outcome:

Cost-effectiveness (if possible):

Relevancy (did the intended audience participate?):

Conclusions (should it be done again? why?):

Did your lesson/intervention change ...

Physical health and well-being ☐

Knowledge? ☐

Attitudes? ☐

Behaviours? ☐

Emotional health and well-being ☐

Did it promote development emotionally, creatively, intellectually and spiritually? ☐

Did it initiate and develop mutually satisfying personal relationships? ☐

Did it allow the pupils to face problems safely, resolve them and learn from them? ☐

Did it develop confidence and assertiveness skills? ☐

Did the children begin to become aware of others and empathise with them? ☐

Did it include play and having fun? ☐

Did the children laugh? ☐

Social health and well-being ☐

Did pupils feel a sense of membership/belonging? ☐

Did children feel they have influence/ability to effect change? ☐

Did children develop shared values? ☐

Did children develop shared emotional connections? ☐

Did it include multi-sensory methods of teaching: ☐

Visual? ☐

Auditory? ☐

Kinaesthetic? ☐

Reassessing the School Health Needs: The School Community

To be completed by the team

Item	Numbers (%)	Where to get information
Number of male pupils on the register		School records
Number of female pupils on the register		School records
Number of white pupils on the register		School records
Number of Afro-Caribbean pupils on the register		School records
Number of South Asian pupils on the register		School records
Number of other ethnic pupils on the register		School records
Number of pupils on the register with a physical disability		School records
Number of pupils on the SEN register		SENCO
Number of pupils with English as a second language		School records
Number of pupils with two parents/carers at home		School records
Main reasons for attendance at A&E		Three-month tally of A&E slips: school nurse
Headteacher's perceptions of main health issues		Headteacher
PSHE coordinator's perceptions of main health issues		PSHE lead

Reassessing the School Health Needs: The School Community

Item	Numbers (%)	Where to get information
School nurse's perceptions of main health issues		School nurse
Pupils' perceptions of main health issues		Ask 2/3 pupils from each year
Parental perceptions of main health issues		Ask parents
Number of obese/ overweight pupils		School nurse
Numbers of pupils eligible for free school meals		School records
Numbers of pupils taking school meals		School records
Parental involvement methods		Headteacher

Reassessing the School Health Needs: The School Environment

To be completed by the assessment team

Item	Numbers (%) information or yes/no	Where to get information
Number of toilets		School walk round
Number of hand washing facilities		School walk round
Are there facilities for the physically impaired?		School walk round
Is there sanitary towel provision for pupils?		School walk round
Description of locality around school (type of road, ease of access, etc.)		School walk round
Description of school grounds (any broken areas, health hazards, grassy areas, positive health areas)		
Healthy school award attained or aiming towards?		NHSP coordinator HT
Number of pupils and staff who walk to school		School count 2 mornings
Number of pupils and staff who cycle to school		School count 2 mornings
What exercise opportunities are there?		School
Is fast food provided?		School cook
Number of vending machines selling sugary drinks/chocolates, etc.		School
Types of healthy snacks available		

Reassessing the School Health Needs: The School Environment (cont.)

Item	Numbers (%) information or yes/no	Where to get information
Average number of fruit portions not consumed per week		Assess numbers left each day for one week
Average number of pupils eating fruit in packed lunch		Assess contents of lunchboxes over 2–5 days
Is water available in school at all times for pupils to drink?		School walk round

School Health Promotion Summary of What Was Done

To be completed by the assessment team

1. What were the three main reasons identified why pupils at the school attended hospital?

2. What health promotion activities did you undertake to address each of these?

3. What are the main environmental issues which need addressing and how did you achieve this?

4. Did the health perceptions differ between pupils, parents, teachers, nurse and headteacher? How was this addressed? Were there areas of commonality?

Reflection on the School Health Promotion Plan

To be completed by the assessment team

Aims:

Short-term objectives (what you aim to achieve by next term):

- raising awareness and providing information (health education)?
- behavioural change support?
- providing supportive environments to enhance positive choices and practice?

What themes (NHSP) will the activities cover and how could they contribute to whole-school improvement?

	Areas of whole-school improvement									
Theme	1	2	3	4	5	6	7	8	9	10

Why was this important?

Methods (how will you do it):

To be completed by the assessment team

Medium-term objectives (what you aim to achieve in two terms):

- raising awareness and providing information (health education)?

- behavioural change support?

- providing supportive environments to enhance positive choices and practice?

What themes (NHSP) will the activity cover and how could they contribute to whole-school improvement?

	Areas of whole-school improvement									
Theme	1	2	3	4	5	6	7	8	9	10

Why was this important?

Methods (how will you do it):

Reflection on the School Health Promotion Plan

To be completed by the assessment team

Long-term objectives (what did you aim to achieve in one year):

- raising awareness and providing information (health education)?

- behavioural change support?

- providing supportive environments to enhance positive choices and practice?

What themes (NHSP) did the activity cover and could they have contributed to whole-school improvement?

	Areas of whole-school improvement									
Theme	1	2	3	4	5	6	7	8	9	10

Why was this important?

Methods (how you did it):

To be completed by the assessment team

The process – how effective was the way in which the activity was delivered? Could it have been done differently?

The outcomes – awareness, knowledge, attitudes or behaviour? How can you measure this?

The relevance – if voluntary, did people come/attend?

Cost-effectiveness – how much did it cost to deliver the activity? Did it prevent something else being done which might have had more effect?

Did the steering group all think the short-, medium- and long-term aims had been met?

What is the next step?

REFERENCES

Arnstein, S.R. (1969) 'A ladder of citizen participation', *Journal of the American Planning Association,* 35 (4): 216–24.

Cremin, H. (2002) 'Pupils resolving disputes: successful peer mediation schemes share their secrets', *Support for Learning,* 17 (3): 138–43.

Croghan, E. (2004) 'Hygiene Intervention in Early Years'. Unpublished.

Croghan, E. and Johnson, C. (2003) 'Occupational health and school health: a natural alliance?', *Journal of Advanced Nursing,* 45 (2): 155–61.

Denman, S., Moon, A., Parsons, C. and Stears, D. (2002) *The Health Promoting School: Policy, Research and Practice.* London and New York: RoutledgeFalmer.

Department for Education and Employment (1999) *National Healthy Schools Standard Guidance.* Nottingham: DfEE.

Department for Education and Skills (2004a) *Healthy Living Blueprint for Schools.* London: HMSO.

Department for Education and Skills (2004b) *Promoting Social, Emotional and Behavioural Skills in Primary Schools,* Primary National Strategy. London: DfES.

Department for Education and Skills (2005a) *Extended Schools: Access to Opportunities and Services for All. A Prospectus.* London: DfES.

Department for Education and Skills (2005b) *Youth Matters.* London: HMSO. See: http://dfes.gov.uk/publications/youth/.

Department for Education and Skills (2005c) *SRE and Parents.* London: HMSO.

Department for Education and Skills/Department of Health (2005a) *The Common Core of Skills and Knowledge.* London: HMSO.

Department for Education and Skills/Department of Health (2005b) *National Healthy School Status – A Guide for Schools.* London: HMSO.

Department of Health (2002) *Making Best Use of National Healthy Schools Standards – A Guide for PCTs.* London: HMSO.

Department of Health (2004a) *Choosing Health: Making Healthy Choices Easier.* London: DoH.

Department of Health (2004b) *National Service Framework for Children, Young People and Maternity Services.* London: HMSO.

Department of Health (2005a) *National Healthy School Programme: A Guide for Schools.* London: HMSO.

Department of Health (2005b) *Hospital Episode Statistics.* See: http://www.hesonline.nhs.uk/ Ease/servlet/DynamicPageBuild?siteID=1802&categoryID=211&catName=External%20cause (accessed 21 October 2005).

Health and Safety Commission (2002) *Revitalising Health and Safety.* London: HSE.

HM Treasury (2004) *Spending Review.* London: HMSO.

Newman, T. (2004) *What Works in Building Resilience?* London: Barnardos.

Office for Standards in Education (2005) *Guidance for Inspectors (Schools).* London: Ofsted.

Office of National Statistics (1999) *The Mental Health of Children and Adolescents in Great Britain.* London: ONS.

Rowe, N. and Champion, R. (1999) *Young People and Sport: National Survey.* London: Sport England.

Social Exclusion Unit (1998) *Bringing Britain Together: A National Strategy for Neighbourhood Renewal.* London: Social Exclusion Unit.

Stock, B. (1993) *Health and Safety in Schools*, 3rd edn. Surrey: Croner Publications.

US Centers for Disease Control and Prevention, National Center for Health Statistics (1998) *Current Estimates from the National Health Interview Survey, 1995*. See: http://www.cdc.gov/nchs/pressroom/98facts/95curest.htm.

Wardle, H. (ed.) (2005) *Obesity in Children under 11*. London: DoH.

Wolraich, M.L., Wilson, D.B. and White, J.W. (1996) 'The effect of sugar on behaviour or cognition in children: a meta-analysis', *Journal of the American Medical Association*, 274 (20): 1617–21.

World Health Organisation (1986) *Ottawa Charter for Health Promotion*. Geneva: WHO.

World Health Organisation (1995) *Global School Health Initiative*. Geneva: WHO.

Alcohol: Support and Guidance for Schools – see Alcohol Concern:
    http://www.alcoholconcern.org.uk/servlets/doc/224
BRAKE – The Road Safety Charity website:
    http://www.brake.org.uk/
Child Accident Prevention Trust (CAPT):
    http://www.capt.org.uk/
Citizenship curriculum:
    http://www.nc.uk.net/webdav/harmonise?Page/@id=6004&subject/@id=4164
DfES Bullying Pack – Don't Suffer in Silence:
    http://www.dfes.gov.uk/bullying/
Drug Education Forum website:
    http://www.drugeducationforum.org.uk/index.asp
Drugs: guidance for schools:
    http://www.dfes.gov.uk/drugsguidance
Education for Citizenship and the Teaching of Democracy in Schools:
    http://qca.org.uk/7907.html
Every Child Matters – cross-departmental website which brings together the government's policies
    for children:
    http://www.everychildmatters.gov.uk/
Every Child Matters Green Paper:
    http://www.everychildmatters.gov.uk/key-documents/
Framework for PSHE and Citizenship at Key Stages 1 to 4:
    http://www.curriculumonline.gov.uk/Subjects/PSHE
Government response to Hidden Harm Report on Parental Drug Use:
    DoH (2004) *Choosing Health: Making Healthy Choices Easier*. London: TSO
Health and safety: teachers' responsibilities and powers:
    http://www.teachernet.gov.uk/wholeschool/healthandsafety/responsibilities/
Healthy Living Blueprint:
    http://www.teachernet.gov.uk/healthyliving
Milly Dowler website:
    http://www.millysfund.org.uk/
National Children's Bureau:
    http://www.ncb.org.uk/
National Curriculum for PSHE (DfES):
    http://www.nc.uk.net/webdav/harmonise?Page/@id=6016
National Evaluation, Primary School/Primary Care Health Links:
    http://www.wiredforhealth.gov.uk/cat.php?catid=1041&docid=7673
National Healthy School Standard – Drug Education (including alcohol and tobacco):
    http://www.wiredforhealth.gov.uk/cat.php?catid=866&docid=7098
National Service Framework for Children:
http://www.dh.gov.uk/PolicyAndGuidance/HealthAndSocialCareTopics/ChildrenServices/Children
    ServicesInformation/fs/en

Non-statutory guidance on school nurses:
>   DfES/DoH (2006) *Looking for a School Nurse*. London: TSO

NSPCC Inform: The Online Child Protection Resource:
>   http://www.nspcc.org.uk/inform

Ofsted Report on Continuing Professional Development for Teachers in Schools:
>   http://www.ofsted.gov.uk/publications/index.cfm?fuseaction=pubs.summary&id=29

Ofsted Report on Drug Education in Schools (2005):
>   http://www.ofsted.gov.uk/publications

Ofsted Report on Drugs Education in Schools: An Update (November 2002):
>   http://www.ofsted.gov.uk/publications/index.cfm?fuseaction=pubs.summary&id=3016

Ofsted Report on PSHE in Secondary Schools (2005):
>   http://www.ofsted.gov.uk

Parenthood guidance – see Parenthood Education in Schools:
>   http://www.parenthood.org.uk/

QCA Schemes of Work for Drug Alcohol and Tobacco at KS 3 and 4:
>   http://www.standards.dfes.gov.uk/schemes3/

Royal Society for the Prevention of Accidents (RoSPA):
>   http://www.rospa.org.uk/

Safety education guidance:
>   http://www.teachernet.gov.uk/safetyeducationguidance

Sex and relationship education guidance:
>   http://dfes.gov.uk/sreguidance

Sex Education Forum website:
>   http://www.ncb.org.uk/sef/

Smoking, drinking and drug misuse:
>   DoH (2006) *Smoking, Drinking and Drug Misuse Amongst Young People in England*. London: TSO.

SRE and parents:
>   http://www.dfes.gov.uk/sreandparents/

Sure Start:
>   http://surestart.gov.uk/home.cfm

Wired for Health:
>   http://www.wiredforhealth.gov.uk/

World Health Organisation:
>   http://www.who.int/en/

Youth Matters Green Paper:
>   http://www.dfes.gov.uk/publications/youth/

INDEX

Added to a page number 't' denotes a table.

A
abbreviations, xvii–xviii
ability to effect change, 51, 53
absence rates, 31
abuse, suspected, 44
accident books, 30, 33
accidents, 32
anxious behaviour, 44
art, emotional health promotion, 45
assessment
  of emotional difficulties, 46
  importance of preliminary, 10
  of partnership working, 64–7
attention deficit disorder, 44

B
belonging, 44, 48, 50–1, 53
biannual get togethers, 56
bicycle accidents, 32
bullying, 42
bullying clubs, 51

C
carers *see* parents/carers
case studies
  Charles Lane School, 59
  Colin Wood Primary School, 38
  emotional health promotion, 47
  Lady Charlottes Primary School, 30
  St Katie's School, 32
  St Thomas Christopher School, 30
change, influence/ability to effect, 51, 53
Charles Lane School (case study), 59
childhood
  risks to emotional health, 42
  risks to physical health, 31–3, 35
Children's Workforce, 3
Choosing Health (DoH), 1
circle time, 45
citizen participation methods, 59, 60t
citizenship, 49–50
classroom rules, setting, 52

closed questions, xv
Code of Practice for Special Educational Needs, 46
Colin Wood Primary School (case study), 38
collaboration, 59
collective action, 59
Common Core of Skills and Knowledge (DfES), 3
common law principles, pupil's health and safety, 28
community
  defined, 49
  encouraging participation, 49–50
  invoking a sense of in-school, 50–2
  see also wider external community; wider school community
community participatory approaches, 59
'competent' persons, appointment of, 27
conduct disorder, 44
consensus lines, 45–6
contracts, for parents/carers, 56
cooks, 61
cost-effectiveness, evaluating health promotion, 131
creativity, emotional health promotion, 45
crossing patrol staff, 61

D
depression, 44
diets, promotion of healthy, 35, 36
drama, xiv–xv
drowning in water, 33
drug education provision, 39
duty of care, to staff, 28

E
education partners, 60–2
Education (School Premises) Regulations (1999), 28
educational psychologists, 61
emotional difficulties
  assessment, 46
  involving families, carers and other partners, 46